A HISTORY
of
GEORGIA
FORTS

Alejandro M. de Quesada

A HISTORY
of
GEORGIA FORTS

GEORGIA'S LONELY OUTPOSTS

THE
History
PRESS

Published by The History Press
Charleston, SC 29403
www.historypress.net

Front cover: Martello tower. *Courtesy of the National Archives.*
Back cover, bottom: *Courtesy of Fort McAllister State Historic Park.*
All images are by the author unless otherwise noted.

First published 2011
Second printing 2011

ISBN 978.1.60949.192.5

Library of Congress Cataloging-in-Publication Data

De Quesada, A. M.
A history of Georgia forts : Georgia's lonely outposts / Alejandro M. de Quesada.
p. cm.
Includes bibliographical references.
ISBN 978-1-54020-563-6
1. Fortification--Georgia--History. 2. Historic sites--Georgia--History. 3. Georgia--History,
Military. 4. Georgia--History, Local. I. Title.
F287.D3 2011
355.009758--dc22
2011009985

CONTENTS

Acknowledgements   7

Introduction   9

1. Colonial Georgia, 1566–1783   11
2. Antebellum Georgia, 1784–1860   33
3. Civil War Georgia, 1861–1865   61
4. Modern Georgia, 1866–2011   83

Bibliography   149
Index   153
About the Author   157

ACKNOWLEDGEMENTS

I would like to thank the following individuals, institutions and societies that have contributed material and/or assistance in the making of this work possible: John Guss; Pete and Phil Payette; Daniel Brown, park manager, Fort McAllister State Historic Park; Brenda J. Carlan, executive director, Currahee Military Museum (Camp Toccoa); Justin Martin, tourism, welcome center and tourism (Eagle Tavern); Tally Kirkland, ranger (ret.), Fort Pulaski National Monument; Martin Liebschner, site manager, Old Fort Jackson; Fort Frederica National Monument; Fort Yargo State Park (Georgia); Fort King George Historic Site (Georgia); Fort Morris Historic Site (Georgia); Fort Hawkins Commission; Old Fort Jackson and the Coastal Heritage Society; United States Army Signal Corps Museum (Fort Gordon); National Museum of the Infantry (Fort Benning); Sixth Cavalry Museum (Fort Oglethorpe); Friends of the Fort (Fort Hollingsworth); Georgia Historical Society; Mighty Eight Air Force Historical Society; Richmond Hill Historical Society; Tybee Island Historical Society (Fort Screven); New Ebenezer Village Museum; Georgia Salzburger Society; Georgia State Archives; Library of Congress; and National Archives.

INTRODUCTION

The military history of Georgia has always been dear to me. As a child, I frequently visited my grandparents for the summer when they lived in Milledgeville, Savannah and Thomasville. My grandfather was a physician for the Georgia state hospital system, and many of these locations were located on or near former military sites. I remembered visiting these sites and hearing stories from my grandfather's coworkers who were military veterans of World War II and Korea. On weekends, my grandfather used to take me to Fort Pulaski, where I spent hours exploring every nook and cranny.

Then I spent nearly five and a half years in Georgia attending Emory University. During those years, I frequently drove on day trips to the interior of the state to discover lost battle and fort sites. At the same time, I became involved in Civil War living history and participated in most of the 125th anniversary reenactments as well as the many Civil War themed films— including *Glory*—that were being produced in Georgia. I loved volunteering my time as a historical interpreter at Chickamauga National Battlefield Park and Fort Pulaski National Monument. To this day, I still drive through Georgia from my home base of Florida and am still discovering new aspects of Georgia's military past.

While it is nearly impossible to list and describe every military fortification or site in detail because of the constraints laid out in the format of this book, this work will focus on those that readily can be visited or those whose historical importance is of such that they must be covered in detail. Essentially every fort that has existed in Georgia's past can be a book unto itself, and the better-known forts—such as Forts Frederica, McAllister and Pulaski—have volumes written about them. However, this work will be concentrating on the lesser-known forts and military facilities that also contributed considerably toward Georgia's military history.

The individual fortifications and military facilities are placed in chapters based upon the era of when these sites were created and not necessarily the period of an event that they were part of. So locations such as Fort Pulaski would be listed in the antebellum era because of the year of its construction despite the fact that its historical importance was during the Civil War. Therefore, *A History of Georgia Forts: Georgia's Lonely Outposts* must be regarded as a primer for any wishing to learn and expand their knowledge on the history of fortifications, defenses and other military facilities in Georgia. A bibliography has been added for those wishing to learn more about the forts mentioned in this work. I hope that the information compiled in this book will be of use and that it will stir those to go off to explore this state's wonderful heritage—regardless of whether it's hidden or out in the open. For it is the hunt for knowledge of what was, what is or what will be that makes it worthwhile.

Chapter I
Colonial Georgia,
1566–1783

Early Spanish Fortifications

The earliest European presence in what is now Georgia was by the Spanish, beginning with San Miguel de Gualdape (1526–27), where approximately 600 colonists, including a few women and some black slaves, and 1 Indian guide, as well as horses and supplies, for three months sailed from Santo Domingo (Hispaniola) in two ships under the leadership of Lucas Vásquez de Ayllón. The Spaniards landed in Winyah Bay, South Carolina (Cabo de San Nicolás), repaired their ships and then headed southwest for forty to forty-five Spanish leagues to find a suitable settlement site near or on St. Catherines Island. Only 150 people made it through the winter and several Indian attacks and returned to Santo Domingo the following spring. The St. Catherines Island Presidio (1566–97, 1605–80) was the earliest European fort that protected the Spanish Franciscan Mission Santa Catalina de Guale (1595), which became the provincial headquarters of Guale (present-day north coastal Georgia). It was destroyed by Indians during the 1597 Guale Rebellion and not rebuilt until 1605. The Spanish fort was later attacked and destroyed by South Carolina forces in 1680. The Spaniards abandoned the presidio for Sapelo Island. The site of the Mission Santa Catalina de Guale is on Wamassee Creek, which has been excavated. Near South Newport was the Tolomato Presidio (1595–97, 1605–84), which defended the Spanish Franciscan mission-presidio Nuestra Señora de Guadalupe de Tolomato. It was probably originally located on the South Newport River near Harris Neck. It burned in 1597 and was rebuilt in 1605, possibly at or near the

Tupiqui-Espogache site. The last Spanish fortification built in Georgia was the Sapelo Island Presidio (1605–84) in the Sapelo Island State Wildlife Management Area. This Spanish presidio protected the Franciscan Mission de San José de Zapala on the north end of the island along Blackbeard Creek. The presidio was destroyed by South Carolina forces. The Spanish garrison abandoned the Sapelo Island Presidio for Amelia Island, Florida.

Fort King George

Fort King George was the first fort on Georgia soil built by the English. It was erected by the colony of South Carolina in 1721, twelve years before the Georgia colony was founded, on the site of the old Fort King George, built in 1721 by Colonel John Barnwell of South Carolina under British royal orders. This tiny cypress blockhouse, twenty-six feet square, with three floors and a lookout in the gable from which the guard could watch

This is the oldest English fort remaining on Georgia's coast. From 1721 until 1736, Fort King George was the southern outpost of the British Empire in North America. A cypress blockhouse, barracks and palisaded earthen fort were constructed in 1721.

over the Inland Waterway and St. Simons Island, was flanked by officers' quarters and barracks, and the entire area was surrounded on all but the river side by a moat and palisades. Garrisoned by his majesty's Independent Company, with replacements of colony scouts, the fort was occupied for six years. During that time, more than 140 officers and soldiers lost their lives here and were buried on the adjacent bluff. The first of the British eighteenth-century scheme of posts built to counteract French expansion in America, Fort King George was also a flagrant trespass upon Spanish territory, and during its occupation, Spain continually demanded that it be destroyed. The troops were withdrawn to Port Royal in 1727, but until Oglethorpe arrived in Savannah in 1733, South Carolina kept two lookouts at old Fort King George.

This fort served as a barrier against the Spanish in Florida, the French in the interior and their Indian allies for about a decade. Soldiers who died in service are buried nearby in a graveyard that was lost for two hundred years. Some of the graves are marked now. Others are on the site of a sixteenth-century Spanish mission. The Fort King George State Historical Marker is located on U.S. 17 on the northeastern end of the Darien River bridge, in Darien, Georgia (McIntosh County).

Fort Argyle

The Georgia colony was formed in 1732, and settlers arrived from England to establish the town of Savannah in February 1733. Other small settlements, such as Abercorn, Josephstown, Thunderbolt and Skidaway, followed within months of James Oglethorpe's arrival. Major settlements, such as Augusta, Darien, Ebenezer and Frederica, followed a few years later. Spain and France were the major threats to Georgia. Creek Indians, loyal to the Spanish, and Cherokee, loyal to the French, were the immediate threat to colonial Georgia. The French, whose stronghold was at Fort Toulouse on the Coosa River in what is now central Alabama, never attacked the tidewater sections of Georgia but were enemies nevertheless.

There were at least two forts, and possibly a third, that were constructed at the Ogeechee River. The first Fort Argyle was completed in the fall of 1733, when England was at peace with its adversaries. This fort was a very small square enclosure with projecting corner bastions and was defended by four cannon. It probably had a strong two-story central blockhouse built on many wooden piers, but its exact dimensions are not known. It may have been similar to the blockhouse at Fort King George, an earlier fort on the Altamaha River, which was about twenty-seven feet square. The buildings associated with the first fort lacked brick. If they had chimneys, they were probably constructed of sticks and mud.

The second Fort Argyle was built in 1742 or 1743 at the height of King George's War. This fort was a square enclosure measuring 110 feet on each side. It was considerably larger than the earlier fort, although it may have lacked the corner bastions and central blockhouse seen on the first fort. Instead, the central part of the second fort may have served as an open parade ground. Brick for chimneys became available for the first time. A barracks building, composed of at least two rooms, was located along the eastern wall of the fort, on the bank of the Ogeechee River. This barracks had a large H-style brick chimney used for heating and cooking. The Spanish made a concerted effort to wipe out Georgia in 1742, but with the aid of Fort Argyle's Rangers, they were repulsed at the Battle of Bloody Marsh on St. Simons Island. The Georgia Rangers were a mix of English, first-generation Americans, Germans, Scots, South Carolinians and Virginians who held down the fort at Argyle in the name of the British Crown. They kept the fort operating from 1733 to 1767. A third rebuilding of the fort occurred in the 1760s during the French and Indian War. This was a time when the largest number of Rangers were garrisoned at Fort Argyle.

The archaeological team suspected that this fort was larger than the previous fort, although very little is known about it. The barracks built during the previous construction phase probably continued to be used during this period. This fort was abandoned in 1767 when the Georgia Rangers were dismissed by General Thomas Gage, commander in chief of his majesty's forces in North America. The fort ruins were found in 1985 by a team of archaeologists with Southeastern Archeological Services on property that now comprises Fort Stewart.

Fort Frederica

Since establishing a colony in 1733 and to forestall any Spanish attempt to regain the Georgia land, General Oglethorpe pushed south from Savannah, exploring the coast, where he selected St. Simons Island for a new fortification. The site, sixty miles south of Savannah, would become the military headquarters for the new colony. Here, in 1736, he established Fort Frederica, named for the Prince of Wales, Frederick Louis (1702–1754). The

Remains of the magazine and building foundations of Fort Frederica.

Remains of the entrance of the barracks within the grounds of Fort Frederica National Monument.

"k" was changed to an "a" because a South Carolina fort had already been named in honor of the prince. Thereby, the feminine spelling was added to distinguish it from the fort of the same name.

Fort Frederica combined a military installation (a fort) with a settlement (the town of Frederica). Due to the Spanish threat only seventy-five miles away, General Oglethorpe took measures to fortify both, surrounding the entire forty-acre area with an outer wall. This consisted of an earthen wall called a rampart that gave protection to soldiers from enemy shot and shell, a dry moat and two ten-foot-tall wooden palisades. The wall measured one mile in circumference. Contained within this outer defense perimeter was a stronger fort that guarded Frederica's water approaches. Designed in the traditional European pattern of the period, the fort included three bastions, a projecting spur battery now washed away, two storehouses, a guardhouse and a stockade. The entire structure was surrounded in a manner similar to the town by earthen walls and cedar posts approximately ten feet high. The fort's location on a bend in the Frederica River allowed it to control approaches by enemy ships. A visitor in 1745 described it as "a pretty strong fort of tabby, which has several 18 pounders mounted on a ravelin (triangular embankment) mounted in its front, and commands the river both upwards and downwards. It is surrounded by a quadrangular rampart, with four bastions of earth well stocked and turned, and a palisade ditch."

Frederica town followed the traditional pattern of an English village. Similar in style if not in scale to Williamsburg, Virginia, its lots were laid out in two wards separated by a central roadway called Broad Street. Each house occupied a lot sixty by ninety feet. Lots had room for gardens, and settlers were given additional acreage elsewhere on the island for growing crops. The first shelters at Frederica were called palmetto bowers. These involved wooden branches covered with palmetto leaves, which, while lacking amenities of a more permanent structure, proved adequate for providing shelter from the sun and rain. In time, many settlers replaced their bowers with more substantial structures than these, but nothing more than foundations remain today. Frederica was never intended to be self-sufficient. Even before the settlers left England, the trustees had provided that adequate stores be furnished for their needs. These were distributed to the townspeople on a regular basis.

Nevertheless, the settlers were also not expected to remain idle. General Oglethorpe had banned slavery from the colony for that very reason. Although the trustees' involvement was purely philanthropic, it was expected that the colonists would prosper by producing wine, silk or some other commodity. General Oglethorpe imported five thousand mulberry trees to try to encourage silk production, but with no success. As an economic venture, Frederica failed as well as Georgia.

Lacking sufficient numbers of soldiers, General Oglethorpe returned to England in 1737 to raise a regiment of redcoats. He was given the Forty-second Regiment of Foote, now known as "Oglethorpe's Regiment," consisting of 250 men from Gibraltar, 300 men recruited in England and 45 men from the Tower of London. These, combined with the soldiers already in Georgia, placed nearly 1,000 men under his command. Returning from England, the regiment fell in for the first time on September 28, 1738. General Oglethorpe's foresight proved fortunate. A year after the regiment arrived at Fort Frederica, Great Britain declared war on Spain. This started a nine-year struggle known in Europe as the War of the Austrian Succession and in America as King George's War. In the Southeast, General Oglethorpe made the first move and launched an attack against St. Augustine of Spanish Florida. Although equipped with sufficient men and supplies, General Oglethorpe's siege failed, and the impregnable Castillo de San Marco remained in Spanish control. The British forces retreated northward, but General Oglethorpe understood that whatever respite they had gained would be temporary.

The Spanish response came two years later. A fleet with thirty-six ships and two thousand soldiers sailed from St. Augustine and arrived off St. Simons Island early in July. The ships forced a passage of Jekyll sound, following a lengthy cannonade with Fort St. Simons. Little damage was done to the Spanish fleet, and the soldiers landed unopposed at Gascoigne Bluff, near where the causeway is today. There, they proceeded to march overland and capture Fort St. Simons without further resistance. The British garrison there evacuated before the Spanish soldiers arrived and retreated north to Fort Frederica.

Despite his initial success, the Spanish commander, Manuel de Montiano, proceeded captiously. He sent a reconnaissance in force of two hundred men up the military road in the direction of Fort Frederica. Before they arrived outside the gates of the town, General Oglethorpe took the offensive. He sent a column of his own troops out to meet the Spanish in the wooded thickets east of Frederica. At a spot where the road crossed a sluggish stream named Gully Hole Creek, the British sprung their trap, firing a volley of bullets into the lead group of Spanish troops. Caught off guard, the Spanish recoiled in shock and confusion, retreating back toward their compatriots at Fort St. Simons.

The British followed up their victory by pursuing the Spanish. Montiano sent reinforcements to help the first column of soldiers, but these too were caught unawares and ambushed at Bloody Marsh. A regular engagement ensued, lasting about one hour, before the Spanish broke off contact and retreated again. Unsure of the terrain or how many enemy soldiers he faced, Montaino re-embarked his forces, set sail and returned to Florida. Never again would the tread of the Spanish boot break the stillness of Georgia's oak and pine forests.

At the time of the Spanish attack in 1742, about two hundred British troops were stationed at Frederica. Some of the officers and married men lived in their own homes in or near town. Others lived camp-style in clapboard or thatched huts adjacent to the barracks where it had accommodated more than one hundred men. The barracks took the form of a square with rooms surrounding an open parade. Walls were made of tabby one foot thick. Soldiers entered the barracks through a gateway covered by a tower made of double thick tabby. During the 1742 military campaign, the barracks served as a hospital and as quarters for Spanish prisoners of war.

By 1743, nearly one thousand people lived at Frederica. The town enjoyed a relative measure of prosperity owing to the Crown's dispensation, but it was a prosperity that was built on military outlays. For Frederica, the peace treaty that Great Britain and Spain signed in 1748 sounded its death knell. No longer needed to guard against Spanish attack, the garrison was withdrawn and disbanded. The local economy collapsed, and as many as half the town's people left to seek their fortunes elsewhere. Those who remained continued to call Frederica home until 1758. In that year, a fire started, and before the last flame died out, what remained of the town was a blackened, charred ruin. Nature finished the process of reclaiming Frederica, with vines overgrowing the few tabby ruins still standing. In time, little was left but a memory. Interest revived in Fort Frederica in the 1900s. Local residents took a lead in preserving the site as a reminder of America's colonial past. In 1945, Fort Frederica National Monument was established.

WORMSLOE PLANTATION

Noble Jones applied for a lease for five hundred acres on the south side of the Isle of Hope in 1736 (the trustees didn't approve the lease until 1745) and began building a fortified house overlooking the Skidaway Narrows. The house was constructed between 1739 and 1745 using wood and tabby, a crude type of concrete made from oyster shells and lime. The fortress consisted of eight-foot-high walls with bastions at each of its four corners.

Model showing a reconstruction of how the fortified Wormsloe Plantation appeared after construction began in 1739.

Remains of the tabby ruins that made up the colonial-era Wormsloe Plantation. Seen here is one of the bastions of the plantation's fortification.

The fort house was one and a half stories and had five rooms. Oglethorpe allotted Jones's fort a twelve-man marine garrison and a scout boat with which to patrol the river. "Wormslow"—the name Jones gave to his Isle of Hope estate—probably refers to Wormslow Hundred, Herefordshire, in the Welsh border country from which the Jones family hailed. Although some have stated that the name refers to Jones's attempts to cultivate silkworms at the plantation, the fact that Jones's son Noble Wimberly Jones named his plantation Lambeth after his birthplace on the south bank of the Thames, opposite London, lends credence to the former theory.

Noble Jones's fortified house was one of several defensive works built between Frederica on St. Simons Island and the Savannah town site. The English were concerned that the Spanish still claimed the area and would eventually attempt to expel them. Conflict finally erupted in 1739 with the outbreak of the War of Jenkins' Ear, which was the name for the regional theater of the greater War of the Austrian Succession. Jones took part in an English raid along the St. Johns River in northern Florida in 1740 as well as the successful defense of Frederica at the Battle of Bloody Marsh in 1742.

The end of the war in 1748 largely neutralized Spanish threats to the new colony. In 1752, when Georgia became a royal colony, Jones received a royal grant for his Wormsloe holdings. His support of the Crown continued as he served on the governor's council and as chief justice, a commander of the militia and treasurer of the colony. His loyalty to the king continued despite his son's ardent support of the Patriots as the Revolution neared. Noble Jones's death in 1775 saved his family from the open conflict that marked so many Georgia families when the Revolution began in earnest. His death was probably the last of the original colonists who had arrived aboard the *Anne* some forty-two years before.

With Jones's death, his son, Noble Wimberly, assumed the family's leadership role in Georgia. That position has been maintained by succeeding generations of the family. Descendants of the original family still reside at this site and are actively involved in heritage preservation at Wormsloe. The family's continued participation in civic and community affairs is a valuable contribution today, as in the past.

Today, the state-controlled area includes the scenic oak-lined avenue, a museum and a walking trail that leads through the dense maritime forest to the ruins of the tabby fort built by Noble Jones in 1745. More recently, the park has established a colonial life demonstration area, which includes a replica wattle and daub hut and several small outstructures that simulate a living area for Jones's marines and servants.

FORT BARRINGTON

Approximately ten miles west of the historical marker on Georgia 57 on the banks of the Altamaha River stood Fort Barrington, a stronghold whose origin dates back to the earliest colonial times. It was built as a defense against the Spaniards and Indians and was called Fort Barrington in honor of a friend and kinsman of General James Edward Oglethorpe, Lieutenant Colonel Josiah Barrington. This gentleman, a scion of the English nobility, was a large landowner in Georgia whose home was just east of Barrington Ferry on San Savilla Bluff. Fort Barrington, which was twelve miles northwest of the town of Darien, was renamed Fort Howe during the Revolution as it fell into the hands of the British.

The fort ceased to exist long ago, but the old military road that formerly ran between Savannah and Fort Barrington is still known as the Old Barrington Road. Barrington Ferry, an important ferry since colonial days, was in use until the early years of the twentieth century. The Fort Barrington State Historical Marker is located on Georgia 57 several yards from the McIntosh County line and 3.7 miles north of Townsend, Georgia. This marker is located in Long County, twelve to fifteen feet from the McIntosh County line. Apparently, the Georgia Historical Commission thought it was in McIntosh County and incorrectly used a marker number for McIntosh County.

FORT AUGUSTA—FORT CORNWALLIS

This site was selected by fur traders Kennedy O'Brien and Roger de Lacy as a trading post to be nearer the Indians than Savannah Town (in present Beech Island). To protect them and others, General Oglethorpe in 1735 built here Fort Augusta (so named after a royal princess), maintaining a garrison until 1767. Here he met chiefs of the Chickasaws and Cherokees in 1739 to pacify them after a smallpox epidemic. In 1750, the first St. Paul's Church was built "under the curtain of the fort." In 1763, chiefs of the Cherokees, Creeks, Catawbas, Chickasaws and Choctaws met here with governors of Georgia, North and South Carolina and Virginia and the king's representative and signed a treaty of peace. Again, in 1773, Cherokees and Creeks here ceded two million acres in North Georgia.

During the Revolution, the British on this spot erected Fort Cornwallis, which was captured by the Americans by surprise on September 14, 1780,

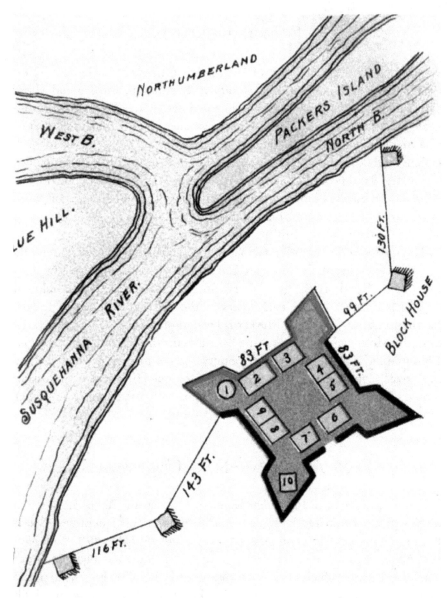

A period map showing the fortifications and defenses of Fort Augusta during the American Revolution. *AdeQ Historical Archives.*

but soon abandoned to the British. In May 1781, an attack under General Andrew Pickens and Lieutenant Colonel "Light Horse Harry" Lee, and the use of a Mayham tower, forced surrender by the British commander, Lieutenant Colonel Thomas Brown, with capitulation taking place on June

The only remnant associated with the fort is one of its cannons that was turned into a memorial on the actual site in modern Augusta.

5, 1781. In 1786, fortifications were removed and a new church was built by the trustees of Richmond Academy for use by all denominations. In 1818, the site was conveyed to the trustees of the Episcopal church, who constructed a new St. Paul's Church, which was destroyed in the 1916 fire and replaced by the present structure. The Fort Augusta–Fort Cornwallis–St. Paul's Church State Historical Marker is located at Sixth and Reynolds Streets in Augusta (Richmond County).

Fort Darien

Fort Darien, laid out by General James Edward Oglethorpe in 1736, was built on this first high bluff of the Altamaha River to protect the new town of Darien. It was a large fortification, with two bastions and two half bastions, and was defended by several cannon.

From the time of its settlement by Scottish Highlanders in 1736 until after the Battle of Bloody Marsh in 1742, the town of Darien was in constant danger from the Spaniards of Florida. Often for weeks at a time, the Highland soldiers were absent from home on military campaigns, with only a few men left to guard the women and children who, for safety, lived within the walls of the fort. On several occasions, the post was fired upon by Spaniards or their Indian allies. After the war with Spain was ended, the fort, no longer needed, fell into ruins but was rebuilt and armed during the Revolution, when it again saw action, this time against British forces. The Fort Darien State Historical Marker is located on U.S. 17 on the northeastern end of the Darien River bridge, in Darien, Georgia (McIntosh County).

Fort McIntosh

Near the town of Atkinson, on the northeast side of the Satilla River, Fort McIntosh was built early in the Revolutionary War to protect extensive herds of cattle ranging between that river and the Altamaha. It became an important post on the southern frontier. The fort, a small stockade one hundred feet square with a bastion at each corner and a blockhouse in the center, was garrisoned by forty men from the Third Carolina Regiment and twenty Continentals from the Georgia Brigade, under command of Captain Richard Winn. On February 17, 1777, a large force of Tories and Indians, commanded by Colonel Brown, Colonel Cunningham and Colonel McGirth, attacked Fort McIntosh, besieging it for more than twenty-four hours.

Captain Winn refused all demands for surrender until there was no longer hope for reinforcements from Fort Howe and he was forced by superior numbers to evacuate the post. Under terms of surrender, a British company was to escort the Georgia troops to the Altamaha to protect them from massacre by the Indians. These terms were not honored, and Captain Winn and his small company marched unguarded by night through the dense forest and swamp to Fort Howe. The Fort McIntosh State Historical Marker is located at the intersection of U.S. 82 and Georgia 110 in Atkinson, Georgia (Brantley County).

Ebenezer Revolutionary War Fortifications

The town of Ebenezer was established by a colony of German-speaking Lutheran refugees in 1736 and was laid out on an identical plan to that of Savannah, with a rectangular grid of town lots that were regularly broken up by public squares, streets and lanes. It contained approximately 160 town lots, of which fewer than 100 were likely occupied. The most heavily settled areas were nearer to the Savannah River. Besides the homes, the plan included a church, a parsonage, an academy, an orphan house, a public storehouse and market places.

Ebenezer served as a major military headquarters for the British and Loyalist forces under command of Major General Augustin Prevost. The town served as a bivouac and campaign staging areas as well as containing large military garrisons for both sides of the conflict. Ebenezer hosted a military hospital. The British and Loyalists who were garrisoned at Ebenezer were a sickly lot. Their plight is partly documented in a surgeon's account

The remains of one of the redoubts that made up the Revolutionary War–era fortifications of the town of Ebenezer.

that was published as *The Fevers of Jamaica*. Ebenezer also had its "Great Swamp Hospital," which was operated by the Patriots in 1782.

A military prison existed in the town, although it was considered a temporary facility. Ebenezer held captured Loyalist Native Americans for a brief period in 1782. Many hundreds of soldiers from both sides of the conflict died and were buried at Ebenezer. Ironically, none of their grave sites is known. The town, in addition, contained a large storage depot for military supplies, including weapons, ammunition and accoutrements. As fears of an invasion by sea grew in Savannah, large stores of the Patriots' precious munitions were shifted to safer location at Ebenezer. The British also kept munitions at Ebenezer during their occupation. The handsome brick Jerusalem Church was used first as a hospital for sick and wounded soldiers and later as a stable for cavalry horses.

The battle at Ebenezer took place in September 1779 when Brigadier General Casamir Pulaski and his legion attacked the nearly vacant town after most of the British and Loyalists were removed to defend Savannah. A later 1782 engagement, which is chronicled in Heitman's list of battles, actually is a combination of three different engagements that occurred within the vicinity of Ebenezer.

The British built a series of small forts, or redoubts, which were connected by ditches and abatis lines around the town's perimeter. Most of Ebenezer's fort system was designed and built by the British or enslaved workers. A plan map showing most of these defenses has survived. The Patriots also had some military constructions before and after the British invasion, but the configuration and extent of these defenses is poorly documented. The Continentals and militia under command of Anthony Wayne reoccupied at least some of the British defenses. General Wayne and his troops left Ebenezer in late June or early July 1782 to occupy Savannah. His superior, General Nathanael Greene, wrote to Wayne advising him to level the British fortifications before leaving Georgia. The archaeological evidence from at least two of the Ebenezer forts, Redoubts 2 and 3, and also in the case of the British fortifications at Savannah, indicates that General Wayne followed General Greene's orders. Redoubt 4 at Ebenezer was left completely intact, however, and remains visible today. Its survival can be explained by General Greene's letter to General Wayne, in which Greene ordered that the forts were to be leveled, leaving one for refuge of the citizens should British forces return.

As the town was once more in the hands of the Continentals and the temporary headquarters of General Anthony Wayne, the Georgia legislature assembled there, and Ebenezer became for a short time the actual capital of Georgia. On February 16, 1796, Ebenezer was made the county seat of Effingham and so served until 1799, when the courts were removed to Springfield. The New Ebenezer State Historical Marker is located at the end of Georgia Hwy 275 in Effingham County.

FORT MORRIS

This small cannon was part of the armament of historic Fort Morris at Sunbury during the American Revolution. In November 1778, a superior British force from Florida under Colonel Fuser of the Sixtieth Regiment besieged the fort. To the ultimatum to surrender, the American commander, Colonel John McIntosh, sent back the laconic reply: "Come and take it." The enemy thereupon abandoned the siege and retired southward. In January 1779, the British returned to Sunbury by water. Fort Morris was then under the command of Major Joseph Lane of the

The earthworks of Fort Morris was the site of a series of fortifications built there since 1741 and served the Patriot cause well during the American Revolution.

Continental army. Ordered by his superiors to evacuate Sunbury following the fall of Savannah, Lane found reasons to disobey and undertook to defend the post against the overwhelming British force under General Augustin Prevost. After a short but heavy bombardment, the fort was surrendered on January 9, 1779, with its garrison of 159 Continentals and 45 militia.

This cannon, which was excavated at the site of the ruins of the famous Revolutionary fortification in 1940, stands here as a reminder of America's hard-won struggle to achieve independence. The Fort Morris Cannon State Historical Marker is located at the Liberty County Courthouse in Hinesville, Georgia.

SAVANNAH COLONIAL AND REVOLUTIONARY WAR DEFENSES

As early as 1734, on the northeastern bluff near the city, there existed "a battery of 12 guns on the river…Beside them which 2 block houses at the Angles of the town had each 4 guns." However, the first planned defense for the city of Savannah was an earthen fort originally built by the Georgia Colonial Council in 1760, during the French and Indian War, "on the eastern edge of the city on a bluff overlooking the river." It was named Fort Savannah initially but was later renamed Fort Prevost.

During the American Revolution, the Continental army was not prepared for a British invasion of Savannah. The defenses by this time were in disrepair, and some preparations had been attempted but were inadequate for protection. The Continentals sank hulks of various vessels in the river as obstacles as well as erecting a battery at the trustees' gardens near the location of Fort Prevost, but otherwise, Savannah remained defenseless by military standards. "A battery had been thrown up at the eastern extremity of the city, upon which a few guns had been mounted," but "every other part of the city was exposed." The trustees' battery—referred to by the British as "The Fort"—was erected in 1776 and was only a line battery. Though a wall had been erected around the city, it was of little value, according to Byous's "Fortresses of Savannah."

When the British occupied the city in 1778, this fortification was reinforced with forty-eight cannon and forty-three mortars. Furthermore, Fort Prevost was constructed in a modified star shape with bastions on four sides to protect from river and land attack.

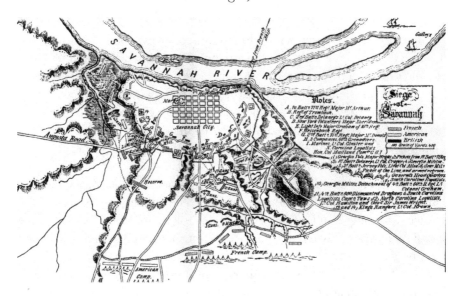

Detailed map showing the British defenses and the siege lines of the Continental army and of the French during the siege of Savannah, 1779. The largest of the defenses of Savannah during the 1779 siege was Fort Prevost. *AdeQ Historical Archives.*

The reconstructed Spring Hill Redoubt that formed part of the British defenses of Savannah and scene of the heaviest fighting during the siege.

Governor Wright ordered up to four hundred slaves to build it. In addition, a magazine was built on the eastern demilune of the fortification. A circle of abatis runs from the western line south and then turns east over the bluff. The abatis consisted of ditches with means of defense formed by felled trees, the ends of whose branches are sharpened and directed outward, or against the enemy. After the Revolution, it was renamed Fort Wayne in honor of General "Mad Anthony" Wayne, the Revolutionary War leader. It soon, however, fell into decay from disuse and disrepair.

Over the ground where the Savannah Visitors' Center is now located, hallowed by the valor and the sacrifice of the soldiery of America and France, was fought on October 9, 1779, one of the bloodiest battles of the Revolution when Savannah, which the British had possessed for several months, was attacked by the combined American and French forces.

A short distance west of the visitors' center stood the famous Spring Hill Redoubt, and along here ran the line of entrenchments built by the British around Savannah since December 9, 1778. After a three-week siege, the allies stormed the enemy works in this area early on October 9. Arrayed in the opposing armies that day were soldiers of many lands—American Continentals, grenadiers of Old France, Irishmen in the service of King Louis XVI, Polish lancers, French Creoles and Negro volunteers from Haiti fighting for American independence against English redcoats, Scotch Highlanders, Hessians, Royalist provincials from New York, Tory militia, armed slaves and Cherokee Indians.

After a heroic effort to dislodge the British, the allies retired with heavy losses. Thus the siege was lifted, and the French fleet sailed from Georgia, ending an episode of far-reaching significance in the American Revolution. The "Attack on British Lines" State Historical Marker is located at the Visitors' Center at West Broad and Liberty Streets in Savannah, Georgia (Chatham County). In addition, a reconstruction of the Spring Hill Redoubt was built in 2007, thereby reconnecting the city with its revolutionary past.

From the earliest days of the founding of the colony there began a series of measures protecting the entrances toward as well as the outskirts of the city of Savannah. Jones's Narrows was a major inland waterway that flowed past the Wormsloe plantation of Captain Noble Jones. A temporary timber guardhouse was built in 1739 and 1740 as protection. Thomas Jones, the treasurer of the colony, was allotted 27 British pounds, 18 shillings, 6 pence to cover the "charges of Building a Guard House on Pine Island Near Skidaway Narrows" on September 29, 1740. With this allotment, a tabby fortification, Fort Wimberly, was constructed to replace it. In addition, fortifications were built by the British in Hardwick to protect Savannah's "back-door." There, a fort was erected on the "northeast angle of the town, two hundred feet square." Another fort at the northwest angle was built and paid for personally by Governor Henry Ellis, costing £400 British, and was 120 feet square.

The most important of the forts that protected the outskirts of Savannah was Fort George. John DeBrahm, the surveyor general of the Southern District of North America, laid out and supervised the construction of Fort George on Cockspur Island in the mouth of the Savannah River in late 1761. Construction of the fort began in the following spring.

It was a small, embrasured redoubt, one hundred feet square, with a blockhouse or bastion forty feet square and thirty feet high to serve as a barracks and storehouse, magazine, adequate to accommodate fifty men, "more to stop vessels from going up and down in time of peace, than vessels which had a mind to act in a hostile view." In November 1762, the assembly ordered improvements on the fort consisting of brickwork and palmetto puncheons around the perimeter of the earthworks. The fort was armed with eleven guns and four mortars.

In January 1763, the governor ordered the fort be notified that all ships coming from Charleston must be quarantined for ten days. At a time when Fort George was considered to be in total ruin, there were only three men and one officer serving as garrison "just to make signals" in the spring of 1772. The fort was completely dismantled in 1776 to deprive the British of any benefits it might offer, and its guns were removed to Savannah, where they could aid in the defense of the city.

Chapter 2
ANTEBELLUM GEORGIA, 1784–1860

FORT WAYNE

After the American Revolution, Fort Wayne fell into disrepair. In 1806, foreseeing a future conflict between England and the United States, the city council of Savannah ceded to the United States government the site of Fort Wayne—which had evolved from the previous Fort Prevost after the American Revolution—in hopes that the federal government would expand the defenses of the city. Over the next two years, the government acquired numerous private parcels for construction of a large fortification; however, the government did not follow through with that project, and the city undertook the strengthening of Fort Wayne on its own.

Fort Wayne had been reduced in size since 1780, eliminating the southern and eastern outer works and reconfiguring the western wall. A crescent-style structure was finished by 1813, and the city was walled by the end of 1814. By 1824, Fort Wayne was out of date. Bought by the Savannah Gas and Light Company in 1852, all indications of the previous fortresses were gone. The brick buttress of the gasworks that still stands today covers only a portion of the fort's area.

In all probability, the reasoning of the Army Corps of Engineers was that Fort Wayne was too close to the city to provide adequate protection for Savannah. After all, in 1779, during the unsuccessful Franco-American siege of the British-held city, French warships anchored in Five Fathom Hole, the future site of Fort Jackson, had shelled the city. What was needed was a defensive position farther away and downriver from the city.

Fort Wayne was built on the site of Fort Prevost in the early nineteenth century. Today, the only remnants of the fort are the buttressed brick walls that made up the base of the fort and the buildings of the Savannah Gas and Light Company.

This battery formed part of the defenses of Savannah during the War of 1812. It is located in Emmet Park near the end of East River Street.

FORT EDWARDS (EAGLE TAVERN)

In 1789, the building was used as a blockhouse defense against the Cherokees and was called Fort Edwards. An intermediate building probably existed on the site, incorporating at least part of the old fort. The Eagle Tavern in its present form was built in 1820 along a stagecoach route that carried students north to the University of Georgia. The tavern was a popular stop with the students and gained somewhat of a reputation.

This inn/tavern/stagecoach stop has been restored to look the way a frontier tavern might have looked in early nineteenth-century Georgia. However, it is currently believed by local historians that the inn may have been a fort during the 1700s. The Oconee County Tourism Department manages the Eagle Tavern and is located across from the courthouse in Watkinsville, the county seat of Oconee County.

The Eagle Tavern was built before 1801 and possibly as early as 1794 when Watkinsville was a frontier town on the edge of Creek and Cherokee Indian territories. It is believed by some that this site was once called Fort Edwards and served as a gathering place for early settlers who needed protection from attacks by the many Creek and Cherokee Indians who flourished in this area. The Eagle Tavern is one of the earliest surviving structures in Oconee County.

FORT HOLLINGSWORTH

Georgia's boundaries in the 1700s can best be described as the wild frontier. Between 1782 and 1797, various treaties were made with the Indians to define Georgia's boundaries. Blockhouses and "forts" were built to protect the settlers who lived on the frontier. Indians were likely to be incited by misunderstandings. Horses and farm animals were frequently stolen, and families had to be protected in fortress-type buildings surrounded by wooden fences.

Many of these "forts" were merely blockhouses or fortified buildings/ homes that had been reinforced. Most were made from thick logs and contained in most cases a two-story firing platform whereby defenders could fire from loopholes carved through the logs. Construction of Fort Hollingsworth consisted of the logs and rafters being put together with wooden pegs in the 1793 portion of the building. Rocks and white mud chinking were used to fill the cracks between the timbers.

Fort Hollingsworth was built by Jacob Hollingsworth (circa 1792–93) and appears on a 1793 map of the area. Around 1860, the fort was purchased by the White family, who built an addition to the fort to make it into a typical farmhouse of that era.

Antebellum Georgia, 1784–1860

The lands of the first settlers of Franklin County, whose lands were granted by the State of Georgia between 1783 and 1788, lay north of the Indian boundary fixed by the treaty of 1785. These lands were granted under the impression that they lay south of the agreed boundary line. When this line was surveyed, it was found that these lands lay north of the boundary line in the Cherokee Nation. The Indians demanded their immediate removal.

Fort Hollingsworth–White House was then in the Cherokee Nation. When the boundary lines were redrawn, it was in Franklin County, then in Habersham County and finally in Banks County. William Wofford and Jacob Hollingsworth moved from North Carolina to Franklin County, Georgia, in 1792. The area where they settled was known as Wofford's Settlement. Hollingsworth Fort was first shown on a map of the Defensive Plan Western Frontier, Franklin County, in 1793.

When the line was surveyed and Colonel Wofford learned that their settlement was considered to be in Indian territory, he, along with other settlers in the area, petitioned Georgia governor James Jackson to have the line rerun or to take such action as would be necessary to protect them and their possessions from Indian raids. The Indians ceded a strip of land four miles wide and twenty-three miles long that included Wofford's Settlement. A line of felled trees at least twenty feet wide originally marked the line that became a no-man's land. The United States agreed to pay the Cherokees $5,000 and $1,000 per annum for the property rights. By about 1796, the Indian troubles were about over, and the string of frontier forts were no longer necessary. The forts soon became log farmhouses.

In the following decades, an addition to the two-story single pen that had been the fort was added that made it look like any other farmhouse of the mid-1800s. The addition was linked to the original structure by a covered walkway, known as a dogtrot. In 1903, the fort was passed to the children of Joshua and Katharine Lane White. Lafayette (Fate) and Emma Payne White raised their family there. In 1936, Beacher White, grandson of Josh and Katy White, acquired the property. In 1980, it passed to Beacher and Mellie Segars White's children. Fort Hollingsworth–White House looks very much today as it did in the 1860s. It is listed on the National Register of Historic Places and is operated by the nonprofit organization Friends of the Fort.

Fort Yargo

This remarkably preserved log blockhouse was built in 1793, according to historians. There are several references to Fort Yargo as existing prior to 1800. Its location is given as three miles southwest of "Jug Tavern," the original name for Winder.

Early historians say Fort Yargo was one of four forts built by the Humphries brothers to protect early white settlers from Indians. The other three forts were listed as at Talassee, Thomocoggan (now Jefferson) and Groaning Rock (now Commerce). Fort Yargo is now a state park with recreational facilities. The Fort Yargo State Historical Marker and preserved blockhouse are two miles south of the main entrance to Fort Yargo State Park at the Winder city limit sign on Georgia 81 (Barrow County).

Fort Yargo is one of the few remaining fortified blockhouses still in its original unaltered form.

A rare view of an interior of a fortified blockhouse built for local farming families to escape to from Indian attacks. The image was taken through one of the loopholes of Fort Yargo that the defenders would have fired their muskets through.

FORT MATHEWS

About two miles south of the historical marker, in the fork of the Appalachee and Oconee Rivers, stood Fort Mathews, built in 1793. From this fort, Thomas Houghton observed the activities of General Elijah Clark and his land-hungry followers as they built forts and fortifications for the protection of Clark's "Trans-Oconee-Republic." From here, Houghton wrote to Governor George Mathews the report that led to the arrest of General Clark and the downfall of his dream of an independent republic established on land not yet ceded by the Creek Indians. The Fort Mathews State Historical Marker is located on U.S. 278 on the west end of the bridge over the Oconee River, Greene County.

FORT PETER

Built in 1796 at St. Marys, then the southernmost U.S. city on the eastern seaboard, Point Peter was armed with a battery of eight cannons at the tip of a two-mile-long peninsula less than a mile wide. While defending the coast from invasion, the fort also trained American militiamen. In the War of 1812, which actually lasted until 1815, America waged its last conflict against foreign invaders and settled any doubts about the fledgling nation's permanent independence from Great Britain.

Though the British had signed the Treaty of Ghent on Christmas Eve 1814, officially ending the war, word had not yet spread to commanders in the United States. Two days after Jackson's victory at New Orleans, as many as 1,500 British troops landed on Cumberland Island off the Georgia coast on January 10, 1815. British forces under the command of Admiral Sir George Cockburn landed on Cumberland Island in an effort to tie up American forces and keep them from joining other American forces to help defend New Orleans, Louisiana, and the Gulf Coast. The British force consisted of the three Royal Marines Battalions (560 men in the First and Second, plus the six companies of the Third), ships' detachments of Royal Marines from the squadron (120 men) and two companies from the Second West India Regiment (190 men).

Bad weather and lack of materials and ships delayed Cockburn until it was too late to produce any effect on the outcome of the battle for New Orleans. Despite the U.S. victory at New Orleans, the occupation of Cumberland Island continued. On January 13, a British force first bombarded and then landed near Fort Peter on Point Peter by the town of St. Marys. The British attacked and took the fort without suffering any casualties.

The British land force then headed for St. Marys along the St. Mary's River. While they were on their way, they encountered a small American force of 160 soldiers of the Forty-third Infantry Regiment and the Rifle Corps under Captain Abraham A. Massias. A skirmish ensued before the Americans retreated. Massias estimated the size of the British force as 1,500 men. He reported that American casualties on January 13 numbered 1 killed, 4 wounded and 9 missing. Although Massias believed that British casualties were numerous, they amounted to only 3 men killed and 5 wounded in the entire expedition.

On January 15, the British captured St. Marys. American reports suggest that the British looted the jewelry store and stole fine china and other goods from the residents. British reports are that they agreed to terms with the town's inhabitants under which the residents gave up all public property and the British respected all private property. The British captured two American gunboats and twelve merchantmen, including the East Indiaman *Countess of Harcourt*, which an American privateer had captured on its way from India to London. The British ended their occupation of St. Marys after about a week. They burned the fort, including its blockhouses and barracks, and withdrew to Cumberland Island.

This small battle was the only land engagement during the war to occur within the territory of Georgia. In 1953, a historical marker was placed at the battlefield. As of 2009, archaeologists have found thousands of artifacts, including cannons, muskets, musket balls, knives and uniform buttons.

Fort Benjamin Hawkins

Fort Hawkins was a War of 1812 frontier fort and U.S. Army headquarters complex that operated from 1806 to 1821. It was located in present-day Macon, Georgia. Fort Hawkins was established in 1806 by President Thomas Jefferson and Indian Agent Colonel Benjamin Hawkins as an official U.S. Army fort and Indian factory for trading and meeting with Native Americans. It overlooked the ancient Indian mounds of the "Old Fields" held sacred by the Muskogee Creek Nation, as well as overlooking the Ocmulgee River, the Lower Creek Pathway that became the federal road connecting Washington, D.C., to Mobile and New Orleans and the future site of Macon, founded across the river seventeen years later.

Built in 1806, Fort Hawkins was the supply base for the army in the War of 1812 and served as a trading center prior to the founding of Macon in 1823.

A stockaded fortification, Fort Hawkins consisted of slightly less than an acre and a half of enclosure, surrounded by a much larger area of cleared land. Inside the fort were two three-story blockhouses. The lowest floors were built with stone for storage of food and munitions. These buildings projected from the log walls of the fort, allowing soldiers to sweep all four walls with musket fire in the event of attack. Long log buildings were built along each of the fort's four walls, and an officers' quarters structure was constructed in the center of the fort. In 1807, Fort Hawkins was garrisoned by troops from Milledgeville's Fort Wilkinson.

In early March 1807, Aaron Burr passed by the fort under guard and may have been held overnight in the garrison. Burr was under arrest for treason (for preparing a private army to invade Florida, New Orleans or Mexico or to lead a secession of the western states from the Union) and was in the custody of William R. Boote. Boote was a commander at Fort Wilkinson but was also prominent in the building of Fort Hawkins. The fort was used as a staging area for the War of 1812's Battle of New Orleans as well as the Creek and Seminole Wars. It also played a role in Andrew Jackson's invasion of Spanish Florida during the First Seminole War of 1817–18. Jackson himself visited the fort in February 1818 while on his way to the scene of the fighting on the Georgia frontier. After the frontier moved farther westward and Macon was founded in 1823, the fort was decommissioned in 1828. As the westward push of the settlers negated the effectiveness of the fort, locals began to call the area around the fort "Newtown."

Although it appears that the fort was not garrisoned after 1819, some of the buildings remained standing for decades. One of the blockhouses, in fact, could still be seen at the site as late as 1879. The strategic site of the old fort saw military use again during the Civil War in 1864 when Confederate artillery fired from there in defense of Macon.

From 1928 to 1938, through the efforts of the Macon Kiwanis Club, Daughters of the American Revolution and Works Progress Administration, a replica of Fort Hawkins's southeastern blockhouse was reconstructed on the exact location of the original, using some of the original stones in the basement section. The upper floors were made of concrete formed to simulate the original wood timbers.

During reconstruction in 1936, archaeological studies conducted at the site revealed the location and extent of some of the stockade walls and corner blockhouses. Further archaeological investigations of the fort site were conducted in 1971. These excavations uncovered many everyday items used by the fort's inhabitants. The archaeological site was listed on the National Register of Historic Places in 1977. The City of Macon acquired the historic site in 2002. The replicated southeast blockhouse, which is occasionally opened to the public, is a Macon icon.

Currently, the city of Macon's Fort Hawkins Commission is raising funds to reconstruct the entire 1.4-acre (5,700-square-meter) stockade. Extensive archaeological excavation of the fort was conducted in 2005 and 2006, led by archaeologist Dan Elliott. These excavations revealed not one but two forts, as well as many thousands of artifacts from the fort era (1806–21) that paint a colorful picture of life on the American frontier.

FORT JAMES JACKSON

Fort James Jackson was built by the United States government between 1808 and 1812 to defend the harbor and city of Savannah, Georgia. It is nationally significant as one of only five surviving Second System seacoast fortifications. Most of the Second System forts were so radically redesigned

Fort Jackson near Savannah was constructed between 1808 and 1812. The fort continually served its military purpose until it was purchased from the army by the City of Savannah in 1924.

by later defensive construction that little remains of their original works. Fort Jackson has nearly all of its Second System masonry, original design and function intact. Furthermore, the fort is the only surviving example of a masonry gun battery of that coastal defense system.

In 1808, the United States Government purchased a 2.3-acre parcel of land that was identified as Wharf Lot Number 12 from Nichol Turnbull for $1,800 for the purpose of a new fortification to protect the river approach to Savannah. The site was previously occupied by a "mud fort" constructed in the Revolutionary War, about which little is known. Construction of Fort Jackson began late in 1808 under the direction of Captain William McRee of the U.S. Army Corps of Engineers. This construction continued at different intervals, being interrupted by lack of funds or fear of fever among the workforce, until completion of the fort in 1812.

The fort consists of an irregularly shaped gun battery of earth and brick masonry and is enclosed at its rear by brick walls that include four demi-bastions. The gun platform, facing the Savannah River, is supported by arched brick casemates, which served as storage rooms, offices and cells. Located at the southwest side of the gun platform is a brick powder magazine with gabled roof. On the northeast angle of the barbette is an 1870s concrete and granite sod-covered magazine, which was the only addition to this fort after the Civil War. Along the east and west angles of the parade ground are the foundations of two brick enlisted men's barracks. On the center rear of the parade ground is the foundation of a brick officers' barracks, which was not completed. Both battery and rear walls are fully enclosed by a brick-lined wet moat, which is supplied by a tide tunnel on the northwest face of the counter scarp wall.

The fort was garrisoned by local militia, such as the Chatham Artillery, as well as federal troops during the War of 1812. The fort saw no action during the war. Federal troops and state militia were withdrawn from Fort Jackson in 1815. Until 1845, the Savannah District Corps of Engineers undertook periodic maintenance on the fort in order that it might support Fort Pulaski (built between 1829 and 1847) in the defense of Savannah. In 1845, Congress funded repairs to Fort James Jackson at the start of the conflict with Mexico and "caused the War Department to have the old fort put into a state of readiness."

Fort Jackson was manned by the Confederate army during the Civil War, and following the fall of nearby Fort Pulaski, it successfully repelled a Union assault on October 1, 1862. When the Union army, commanded by William T. Sherman, captured Savannah by land in December 1864, it took Fort Jackson almost immediately. The fort went by the name of Fort Oglethorpe between 1884 and 1905 and was little used by the U.S. military. It was purchased by the City of Savannah in 1924 for park purposes and was fully restored in the 1970s. It was declared a National Historic Landmark in 2000. The fort is preserved and interpreted through the efforts of the Coastal Heritage Society, based in Savannah.

FORT EARLY

Fort Early, built by General Blackshear in 1812, was named for Peter Early, governor of Georgia at that time. It was used by General Blackshear during the War of 1812. On February 13, 1818, General Andrew Jackson and his army arrived at the fort and used it in the campaign against the hostile Seminole Indians of Florida and Creek Indians of Georgia. Nothing remains of the fort. It is believed to have been a stockade like many used in Indian warfare. The site of the fort is owned and marked by the Fort Early chapter of the Daughters of the American Revolution. The Fort Early State Historical Marker is located in Crisp County, Georgia.

FORT PEACHTREE

One of a line of forts hastily constructed during the War of 1812 to control the Creek Indians who were in alliance with the British, Fort Peachtree occupied the summit northeast of the confluence of the Chattahoochee River and Peachtree Creek and overlooked the Creek trading post town of Standing Peachtree. First Lieutenant George Rockingham Gilmer (governor of Georgia, 1829–31, 1837–39) erected the fort in 1814. He later said he had "never seen a fort" up until that time, but as far as anyone knows, his construction was successful, since the strength of the fort was never tested. Sergeant James McConnell Montgomery, one of Gilmer's command of twenty-two, wrote General Andrew Jackson on March 20, 1814, that the site, "on a commanding eminence," provided a "romantic" view of the river, both upstream and down. In July, he described the fort as being "two large hew's logg block houses, six dwelling houses, and one fram'd store hose, one Bridge…and five boats," which cost "the Governor not less the five thousand dollars." (Montgomery later returned to live here. He became postmaster of Standing Peachtree and established Montgomery's Ferry near the fort site.) After the War of 1812, Fort Peachtree was apparently abandoned. No trace

Fort Peachtree was one of many forts built during the War of 1812 and is Atlanta's earliest military site. A reconstruction of the fort was built on the property of the Atlanta Waterworks Pumping Station in Fulton County during the country's bicentennial celebrations.

of the fort remains atop the hill. A historical marker is located in the font yard of a home (Ridgewood Road at Ridgewood Circle), and a replica of the fort was built by City of Atlanta Bureau of Water near the Atlanta Waterworks pumping station as part of the bicentennial celebration (Fulton County).

Fort Daniel

Fort Daniel was completed in 1813 to protect the frontier from Indians aroused by the British during the War of 1812. Presumably named for General Allen Daniel, the fort was garrisoned by the Twenty-fifth Regiment of Georgia Militia. To further protect the settlers, Fort Peachtree was built on the Chattahoochee River, thirty miles away. World-famous Peachtree Road was built to connect these frontier forts. The Fort Daniel State Historical Marker is located on Georgia 124 half a mile south of the junction with Georgia 324, north of Lawrenceville, Georgia (Gwinnet County).

Fort Mitchell

Though considered to be in Alabama, this fort was built by the Georgia militia at a time when Alabama was still a territory and played a major role in Georgia's state history. Fort Mitchell, an important post of the Creek War of 1813–14, was built in what is now Russell County, Alabama, by troops under the command of General John Floyd. Floyd had marched an army of Georgians to the Chattahoochee River as part of a three-pronged attack on the Creek Nation. He built a log stockade on the west side of the river to serve as a base for his operations.

Floyd's army, marching west from Georgia, was one of three forces sent by the United States to subdue the Red Stick movement in the Creek Nation. An internal civil war in the nation had spilled over to involve the whites following battles at Burnt Corn Creek and Fort Mims, Alabama, during the summer of 1813.

Named for Governor David B. Mitchell of Georgia, the original fort was a large rectangular stockade thrown up by Floyd's men as they advanced on Autossee, an important Creek village on the Tallapoosa River. Built on a high hill overlooking the Chattahoochee River, Fort Mitchell served as base for Floyd's movements, and he returned there to allow his wounded men to recover following his successful attack on Autossee.

Though located in Alabama across the river from modern-day Columbus, Fort Mitchell was built on a high hill overlooking the Chattahoochee River by Georgia militia troops during the Creek War of 1813–14.

A second expedition against the Red Sticks was launched from Fort Mitchell in 1814 but nearly ended in disaster when desperate warriors almost overran Floyd's army at the Battle of Calabee Creek. The fort also served as a base for one of the last campaigns of the War of 1812. An expedition led by Colonel Benjamin Hawkins left Fort Mitchell in early 1815 and descended the Chattahoochee River to engage a British force positioned on the Florida line. The campaign ended without fighting, however, when news arrived of the end of the war. The two sides met in peace, and Hawkins and his men, most of whom were Creek warriors, returned to Fort Mitchell.

The military significance of the first Fort Mitchell continued through the First Seminole War of 1817–18. Lieutenant Colonel Duncan L. Clinch led a battalion of the Fourth Infantry Regiment down the Chattahoochee from the fort in 1816 to establish Fort Gaines on the line marking the lands given up by the Creek Nation at the Treaty of Fort Jackson. The men went on to participate in the campaign against the "Negro Fort" on the Apalachicola River during the summer of that year.

Regular and militia troops passed through Fort Mitchell throughout the First Seminole War, and it served as an important staging point for the Creek Brigade led by General William McIntosh, a noted Coweta chief who had also sided with the United States during the Creek War.

The original fort was replaced by a second, smaller stockade during the 1820s. This second Fort Mitchell was an important base during the Creek War of 1836 and became the starting point of the Creek Trail of Tears. In 1836 and 1837, thousands of Creek men, women and children left Fort Mitchell on their long forced march to new homes in what is now Oklahoma.

The fort also played a brief role in the Civil War, even though the fortifications had long since disappeared. Organizing units of Confederate troops mustered on the site before heading off to join the regular army. The site of Fort Mitchell is now a park in Russell County, Alabama. The outstanding historic site features a reconstruction of the 1813 fort, historic burial grounds, a museum housing a fascinating collection of historic carriages, a restored nineteenth-century log home and an impressive visitors' center that offers exhibits, a film and a walk through the history of the site.

FORT GAINES

The boundary line defined in the Treaty of Fort Jackson (August 1814) between the confederated Creek tribes and the United States extended eastward from the mouth of Cemochechobee Creek south of the modern town of Fort Gaines to a point near Jesup, Georgia. Signed by General Andrew Jackson for the United States and Tustennugge Hopoie (Little Prince) for the Creeks, the treaty ceded about twenty-three million acres of land and was intended to separate hostile Indians from British forces in Florida during the War of 1812.

A military garrison, later named Fort Gaines, was established on the Chattahoochee River in 1814 to patrol the buffer against the British and hostile Indians created by the land ceded in the Treaty of Fort Jackson. Benjamin Hawkins, venerable Indian agent to the southern tribes, and troops commanded by Coweta Chief William McIntosh had the task of enforcing General Jackson's prohibition of any Indian entering the newly acquired territory. His orders were that "all persons carrying and bringing lies" to the British would be shot. He believed Oketeyeconne and Hitchiti towns near here were havens for spies.

A reconstructed Fort Gaines gives the visitor a view of the strategic value of the site located on the brow of the bluff just below the confluence of Town Branch with Chemochechobee Creek.

The "Founding of Fort Gaines" historical marker is located on Georgia 39 north of Fort Gaines at East Bank Area on Lake Walter George (Clay County). Within a stone's throw from the historical marker for the first Fort Gaines there is another one marking the site of the second Fort Gaines. In May 1836, the Eighty-eighth Regiment of the Georgia militia built a small fort in anticipation of an attack by the Creek Indians. The steamer *Georgian* had arrived crowded with women and children fleeing from the Indian uprising at Roanoke upriver. The steamer *Anna Calhoun* was pressed for five thousand pounds of bacon and eight barrels of flour in order to feed the refugees and militia. The uprising was quelled before the fighting reached Fort Gaines. This was one of the last major insurgences of the Creeks before their removal to the West.

MARTELLO TOWER

Around 1815, Isiah Davenport was commissioned by the U.S. government to construct a Martello tower on Tybee Island. The fortification utilized wood and tabby, a common local building material at the time, instead of the brick commonly used for the construction of British towers. Also unlike the British towers, the Tybee tower featured gun loops on the garrison floor that enabled muskets to be fired through the walls. In a letter written in 1861, John Screven, who was a principal owner of Tybee at the time, described the tower as "a tabby and wood structure 24 feet wide at the base, 34 feet tall

A Civil War view of the Martello Tower on Tybee Island. It was built in 1815 and torn down with the establishment of Fort Screven.

with walls that were 11 feet 6 inches thick." It was never tested in battle and by the time of the American Civil War was in a state of disrepair.

However, on April 13, 1861, Confederate troops took possession of the island and erected a small earthwork battery around the tower that, in addition, served as a barracks for the troops. The battery was equipped with two eight-inch Columbiads to guard the entrance to the Savannah River. The Martello tower was garrisoned by the First Georgia Regulars under the command of Major William Duncan Smith until July 17, 1861, and later by the First Volunteer Guard of Georgia under the command of Colonel Hugh W. Mercer. By the end of the year, the island had fallen to Federal troops. The tower's earthwork defenses were refurbished, and the tower served as a barracks for the troops garrisoning the island throughout the war.

Its unfamiliar design confused local writers, who often said that the Spanish had built the tower when Georgia was Spain's colony. It was torn down to its foundation and buried when the concrete batteries were constructed for Fort Screven during the era of the Spanish-American War.

The Augusta Arsenal

For a period of 128 years until its abandonment in 1955, a United States arsenal was located on a tract comprising approximately seventy acres. An "arsenal at Augusta" to aid the state in resisting invasion was originally provided for by President George Washington in 1793. In 1816, a U.S. arsenal was established on the Savannah River where the King Mill is now located, but the garrison having been wiped out in 1819 by "black fever," it was removed to this site in 1827 and consisted of two magnificent sets of officers' quarters, an enlisted men's barracks and a storehouse building connected by a loopholed wall.

On January 24, 1861, it was surrendered to Georgia troops, with its garrison of eighty men commanded by Captain Arnold Elzey. During the War Between the States, it manufactured a variety of ordnance for the Confederate army. Confederate president Jefferson Davis charged Colonel George Washington with establishing a powder works that would supply all of the Confederate ground forces. He chose Augusta and built the Confederate Powder Works alongside the Augusta Canal and the Savannah River. It became the second largest powder manufactory in the world, turning out about thirty thousand pounds of powder in a single day. Colonel Rains commanded the powder

The Augusta Arsenal as it appeared in the years prior the Civil War. *AdeQ Historical Archives.*

The headquarters building of the Augusta Arsenal as it appears today.

The inner courtyard of the Augusta Arsenal that is surrounded by a defensive wall with loopholes from which the defenders could fire their muskets. Nearby, the guardhouse has been turned into a small museum on the history of the arsenal.

The only remnant of the Confederate Powder Works in Augusta is this chimney. During the Civil War, the powder works produced approximately seventy-five thousand cartridges per day.

works, the arsenal and other city works that contributed to the war effort. The arsenal also produced cavalry equipment, field gear, bayonet scabbards, and cartridge boxes. In early spring of 1865, the South surrendered, and in May, the arsenal was surrendered to the United States government.

Expanding activities to meet the requirements of the army in subsequent wars increased the number of buildings to a total of 101 at the end of World War II. The war greatly expanded military activities at the arsenal: 50 new buildings were constructed for maintenance and supply of ordnance material and fire control operations. Over one thousand people worked at the arsenal during World War II. It remained in operation until 1955, at which point it was converted to house the junior college of Augusta College.

FORT SCOTT

Occupied from 1816 to 1821, Fort Scott was one of the most significant army posts on what was then the southern frontier of the United States. Constructed by the Fourth U.S. Infantry on the Flint River in today's

Decatur County, Georgia, the fort was the launching point for two significant invasions of Spanish Florida by U.S. troops. A command post for military operations during the First Seminole War of 1817–18, Fort Scott may well have been the most important U.S. military installation of its day.

Originally called Camp Crawford, Fort Scott was established on the lower Flint River by soldiers of the Fourth U.S. Infantry in June 1816. The original log stockade was used as a base for American operations against the so-called "Negro Fort" on the Apalachicola River, and it was to this location that the survivors of that terrible explosion were brought in August 1816. The fort was temporarily abandoned during the winter of 1816–17 but reoccupied the following spring.

The fort, named for War of 1812 hero Winfield T. Scott, immediately became a focal point of controversy when the chief of the nearby Creek village of Fowltown, Eneah Emathla (Neamathla), refused to leave grounds taken from the Creeks by the Treaty of Fort Jackson. Troops from Fort Scott attacked Fowltown on November 21, 1817, launching what became known as the First Seminole War. A second attack followed a few days later, and the Creeks, with their Seminole allies, responded on November 30 by attacking an army boat on the Apalachicola River near Chattahoochee and killing nearly forty men, women and children.

Fort Scott itself was attacked by warriors in December, but by January one of the coldest winters ever recorded in south Georgia forced the fighters of both sides to huddle around their fires. In the spring of 1818, Major General Andrew Jackson arrived at Fort Scott with an army of more than one thousand men. Using the fort as a launching point, he invaded Spanish Florida and destroyed many Creek and Seminole villages while also capturing the Spanish settlements of St. Marks and Pensacola.

In the years after the war, a large garrison was maintained at Fort Scott in the event that additional military force was needed to coerce Spain into transferring ownership of Florida to the United States. This decision proved deadly, but not due to battle. In 1820 and 1821, severe malaria outbreaks struck the soldiers stationed at Fort Scott. At one time, as many as 769 of the 780 men stationed at the fort were reported sick with fever.

It was during this period that some of the men were moved to Camp Recovery, a hospital encampment on a high pine ridge south of the Flint River. It was hoped that the relocation would allow some of the men to recover, but the effort failed, and many died.

The fort's useful years came to an end in 1821 when Florida was transferred from Spain to the United States. The soldiers were sent to Fort Smith, Arkansas, a new fort on a new frontier. Fort Scott was abandoned and allowed to rot away. By the 1880s, when the government decided to permanently mark the burial ground there, nothing at all remained of the historic old fort.

A monument was placed on the site but was removed during the 1950s when Lake Seminole was created by flooding the original confluence of the Flint and Chattahoochee Rivers. It was expected that the site of Fort Scott would be flooded, but it remains well above the waters of the lake. Not developed in any way, the site of the old fort is now covered by forest. Fort Scott is owned by the U.S. government and is protected by the U.S. Army Corps of Engineers. The original 1880s monument can be seen at J.D. Chason Park in Bainbridge, and a highway marker stands across the river at Hutchinson Ferry Landing Park (Wingate's Lodge).

FORT HUGHES

Only occupied by the U.S. Army for a period of several weeks during the fall of 1817, Fort Hughes was nevertheless an important outpost on the Georgia frontier. Established by soldiers from the Fourth and Seventh Infantry Regiments following the Seminole War battle at nearby Fowltown,

Two thirty-four-pounder cannons commemorating Forts Hughes and Scott in a riverside park in Bainbridge. Only the Fort Hughes Monument marks the actual site, while the Fort Scott Monument was placed at Fort Scott during the 1880s to mark the graves of more than one hundred U.S. servicemen known to have been buried there and was later relocated to the nearby city of Bainbridge.

the fort was a small blockhouse and stockade constructed to protect an important crossing point on the Flint River. Early maps identify the small rise in Bainbridge's J.D. Chason Memorial Park as the site of Fort Hughes. The site of Fort Hughes has been preserved for many years by the citizens of Bainbridge. Fort Hughes is marked by a thirty-four-pounder cannon along with another cannon removed from the site of Fort Scott.

CAMP RECOVERY

This medical camp was established on September 15, 1820, by the southeastern army of the United States, headquartered at Fort Scott. It was used as a recuperation area for soldiers who had contracted malaria and dysentery in the swampy environs of the fort. Soldiers considered the fort to be the deadliest military assignment in the country because of numerous illnesses and deaths

A thirty-four-pounder cannon marks the site of Camp Recovery near Recovery in Decatur County. *AdeQ Historical Archives.*

there. The camp was located on a high ridge three miles southeast of Fort Scott. A thirty-four-pound cannon marks the site of the camp and nearby cemetery for the soldiers who perished there. The Camp Recovery Historical Marker is located at the intersection of Booster Club and Recovery Roads, just west of Georgia 310, in southwestern Decatur County.

FORT PULASKI

Named for General Casimir Pulaski, the Polish hero who was mortally wounded at the siege of Savannah in 1779, Fort Pulaski was built in accordance with plans by General Simon Bernard, formerly chief engineer under Napoleon. Begun in 1829 and completed in 1847, the fort was constructed principally under Lieutenant J.F.K. Mansfield. There, Lieutenant Robert E. Lee saw his first service after his graduation from West Point.

Pulaski was never garrisoned until its seizure by Georgia troops in January 1861 to prevent occupation by Federal forces. On April 10, 1862, Federal

Construction of a fort to protect the port of Savannah began in 1829 under the direction of Major General Babcock and, later, Second Lieutenant Robert E. Lee. The new fort would be located on Cockspur Island at the mouth of the Savannah River. In 1833, the new fort was named Fort Pulaski.

While the fort was built during the antebellum period in Georgia's history, Fort Pulaski's fame came from the role it played during the War Between the States. Seen here are field musicians of the Forty-eighth New York State Volunteer Infantry Regimental band. *National Archives.*

Fort Pulaski brought the end of the concept of masonry fortifications that was known up until the time of the Civil War. With the introduction of rifled artillery and improved ammunition, fortifications such as these saw new innovations in building defenses.

batteries on Tybee Island commenced the bombardment of Fort Pulaski. After thirty hours of bombardment, as a result of which the walls were breached and its guns disabled, Colonel Charles H. Olmstead surrendered the fort. The bombardment marked the first effective use of rifled cannon against a masonry fortification and constituted an epoch in military history.

Abandoned by 1885, Fort Pulaski became a national monument in 1924 and was placed under the National Park Service in 1933. The Fort Pulaski State Historical Marker is located on U.S. 80 at the entrance to the park, east of Savannah, Georgia (Chatham County).

FORT BUFFINGTON

A half mile north from the historical marker is the site of Fort Buffington, built in the 1830s by local militia. It was one of about twenty-five stockades in the Cherokee Indian Nation used by federal and state troops during the Cherokee removal in 1838. In May and June 1838, seven thousand soldiers forced more than fifteen thousand Cherokee Indians from their homes and held them in the stockades until removal west could take place. Many Indians from the local area were held at Fort Buffington. As many as four thousand Cherokees may have died while in the stockades and on the eight-hundred-mile journey west. Their ordeal has become known as the Trail of Tears. The Fort Buffington State Historical Marker is located on Georgia 20, five miles east of I-575, in Cherokee County, Georgia.

FORT GILMER

One hundred yards east of the historical marker is the site of Fort Gilmer, built in 1838 to garrison U.S. troops ordered to enforce the removal from this region of the last Cherokee Indians under terms of the New Echota treaty of 1833. One of seven such forts erected in the Cherokee territory, Gilmer was the temporary headquarters of General Winfield Scott, under whose command the removal was effected. The reluctant Indians were brought here and guarded until the westward march began. The Fort Gilmer State Historical Marker is located on Old U.S. 411 four miles north of Carters, Georgia (Murray County).

Chapter 3
CIVIL WAR GEORGIA, 1861–1865

CONFEDERATE BATTERY (JEKYLL ISLAND)

In 1861, Confederate battery positions on Jekyll Island were equipped with one forty-two-pounder gun and four thirty-two-pounder navy guns en barbette, each having about sixty rounds of shot and shell. Casemates, hot shot furnace and magazines are recorded, also. Of greater strength than batteries on St. Simons Island, the earthworks of palmetto logs, heavy timber, sandbags and railroad irons were mounted for the protection of Brunswick.

On February 10, 1862, General Robert E. Lee requested permission from Governor Joseph E. Brown to dismantle the stronghold, as "the inhabitants of the island and Brunswick have removed themselves and property" to inland points. Major Edward C. Anderson removed the guns, sending them to Savannah. On March 9, 1862, Lieutenant Miller of the USS *Mohican* landed a rifle company and marines, hoisting the Union flag over the island. In January 1863, to strengthen fortifications at Port Royal, South Carolina, a Federal force was sent by flatboat to seize the railroad irons. Some of the men who had helped build the defenses guided the detachment to them, and "the men enjoyed demolishing them far more than they had relished their construction." The Confederate Battery State Historical Marker is located on Horton Road, Jekyll Island, Georgia (Glynn County).

Savannah Defenses

During the Civil War, there were several batteries and earthworks constructed by the Confederates in defense of Savannah. There were three lines of defense that were adopted to protect Savannah. The first line of defense extended from Causten's Bluff to the Ogeechee River and embraced Greenwich, Thunderbolt, Isle of Hope, Beaulieu and Rose Dhu. Detached works were also constructed on Whitemarsh, Skidaway and Green Islands. The majority of the defenses were built under the supervision of General Boggs.

William Robertson Boggs was a general in the Confederate States Army during the American Civil War, and he was noted as a civil engineer who constructed the military fortifications that protected some of the Confederacy's most important seaports. In recognition of his efforts in constructing the fortifications that defended Savannah, one of the earthworks was named Fort Boggs. Constructed mostly by slave labor, the fort was located approximately two miles east of the city. It was constructed in a five-point configuration

A historical marker describing the Federal batteries established on Tybee Island during the siege of Fort Pulaski.

A Confederate battery that defended the approaches to Savannah. It is located on Battery Crescent on Whitemarsh Island.

Fort Boggs as it appears today in the golf course of the Savannah Golf Club.

Confederate earthworks found on Skidaway Island near Savannah.

Fort Beauregard and one of its guns as it appeared in this early twentieth-century postcard. It is identified as being in the area of Thunderbolt, Georgia, and may in fact be Fort Thunderbolt. *AdeQ Historical Archives.*

with batteries extending southward. The remains of Fort Boggs is now part of the Savannah Golf Club golf course on President Street.

The largest of these fortifications was Fort Bartow on Causten's Bluff. The fort's armament consisted of "one 8-inch Columbiad, two 8-inch naval guns, two 8-inch Columbiads, two 24-pounder and one 12-pound rifled cannons, two 8-pounder Smoothbore guns, two 6-inch and three 3-inch rifled guns, and one boat howitzer. Another batter in front of Fort Bartow maintained two 32-pounder smooth bore cannons," according to John Walker Guss's *Fortifications of Savannah, Georgia*. Remains of the fort still exist to this day.

Others included Fort Thunderbolt and Fort Tattnall along the Wilmington River. The Thunderbolt Battery consisted of a ten-inch Columbiad, two eight-inch Columbiads, two eight-inch shell guns, one forty-two-pounder rifled gun, one forty-two-pounder smoothbore and six thirty-two-pound field guns. Other nearby batteries were Lawton and Lee (near Fort Jackson). At the junction of the Burnside and Vernon Rivers was Beaulieu Battery, while in the southwest guarding the Little Ogeechee River was Battery Rose Dew. The most isolated of these defenses was Battery Stephens on Green Island, whose brick magazine still stands. Additional remains of Confederate batteries and earthworks are found on Whitemarsh Island and Skidaway Island.

Among the batteries on the Isle of Hope were Battery Daniels, Fort Wimberly and Battery Beaulieu, which guarded the entrances to the Vernon and Burnside Rivers. The Isle of Hope Methodist Church, located at 412 Parkersburg Road, was built in 1859 prior to the start of the Civil War. The grounds were used as a Confederate battery, consisting of two eight-inch Columbiads and two thirty-two-pound cannon. The church was used as a Confederate hospital during the Union occupation of the area in 1864, and the pews, still in existence, were used as beds. Carvings in the pews made by patients are still visible today. General Sherman, who didn't have much respect for organized religion, melted the church bell for cannonballs. A gallery in the back was for slaves. The historic cemetery holds the graves of thirty-three Confederates from Effingham County.

FORT MCALLISTER

Situated at Genesis Point, ten miles east on the right bank of the Great Ogeechee River below the "lost" town of Hardwick, this fort was the right of the exterior line designed for the defense of Savannah. It denied the use of the river to Union vessels, protected King's Bridge (2.5 miles north) and the Savannah and Gulf (ACL) Railroad bridge 2 miles below and preserved

Federal troops manning one of the captured positions of Fort McAllister in Richmond Hill south of Savannah. *Courtesy Fort McAllister State Historic Park.*

One of Fort McAllister's thirty-two-pound cannons as it appears today. Fort McAllister's defenses were formidable; however, it could not sustain the overall might and manpower of the Federal onslaught for any long periods.

the river plantations from Union raids. Built in 1861–62 to guard the "back door" to Savannah, during 1862–63 it repulsed with minor losses seven attacks by armored vessels, some mounting fifteen-inch guns.

Fort McAllister finally fell on December 13, 1864, when attacked from the rear by Hazen's Division, Fifteenth Corps (Union), which passed this point about 7:00 a.m. and marched via Bryan Neck road (Georgia 63). Although its commander, Major George W. Anderson, refused to surrender, all resistance was smothered under waves of Union infantry, which the small garrison of 230 officers and men could not long resist. The fall of Fort McAllister opened the Great Ogeechee River to Union supply ships and enabled General Sherman to establish a base at King's Bridge. From it, he could supply his whole army (about 60,000 men), which, after a three-hundred-mile march from Atlanta, was then closing in on Savannah.

In December 1864, Fort McAllister mounted eleven siege guns, twelve field pieces and one ten-inch mortar. Below it, piles and torpedoes obstructed the channel. As the Union forces neared Savannah, the fort's capture became imperative in order that ships could pass upriver to supply them. Naval attempts having failed, Brigadier General So. B. Hazen's Division, Fifteenth Corps (Union), was ordered to cross the river, move to the fort and take it from the rear.

At dawn on December 13, Hazen crossed at King's Bridge and marched via "Cross Roads" (Richmond Hill) and Bryan Neck road (Georgia 63), arriving about noon. At 4:45 p.m., after a difficult deployment, he assaulted the fort; by 5:00 p.m., his three brigades had swarmed over the works and overpowered individually Major George W. Anderson's small garrison of 230 Georgians, who fought gallantly to the end. General Sherman watched the assault from Dr. Cheves's rice mill, two and a half miles north-northwest across the river, after which he opened communications with Admiral Dahlgren's fleet (Union), waiting in Ossabaw Sound. Losses were, for the Union, 24 killed, 110 wounded, total 134; and for the Confederacy, 14 killed, 21 wounded, 195 captured, total 230.

FORT GAINES

The third and final fort at Fort Gaines was built by Confederate Army Engineers in 1863. One of a series of installations constructed to defend the Apalachicola and Chattahoochee Rivers from Union attack, the fort consisted of two earthen gun emplacements on top of the bluff, a third emplacement

A Confederate battery in Fort Gaines. Seen here is one of three thirty-two-pounder guns that defended the fortifications during the Civil War—of which one still exists in its original location.

at water level below, connecting trenches, magazines and other defenses. A large magazine of lumber and sand was built about sixty feet from the bluff with trenches running north and south to cannon. Breastworks were thrown up along the bluff. John Seals, Dr. James Mandeville, Dr. Gaston and Captain John B. Johnson, a recent graduate of West Point, were among the officers in charge. The fort never came under attack, and Fort Gaines's primary importance during the war years was as a supply and hospital center.

After the Battle of Olustee (Ocean Pond) in northern Florida in 1864, casualties were brought up the river to Fort Gaines, where all available churches, stores and other buildings became temporary hospitals. Most outstanding of these was the Wayside Home in the old Masonic building. At least nine died and are buried at New Park Cemetery. In addition, a number of prisoners, overflow from the prison at Camp Sumter (Andersonville), were brought to Fort Gaines and kept under guard in the yard of the old County Courthouse. The fort and local area were maintained by the Fort Gaines Militia until the end of the war without having been engaged in any action.

The Confederate fort at Fort Gaines is unique among similar installations in that one of its thirty-two-pounder cannon has remained in place for more than 140 years. The gun can still be seen in one of the well-preserved earthworks on the bluff. Historical markers at the site tell the story of both the Confederate and 1836 fortifications.

Camp Sumter (Andersonville Prison)

A formal prisoner exchange system was devised in July 1862. The system was governed by the Dix-Hill Cartel, which specified the worth of each soldier by rank. For example, one captain alone was worth sixty privates. However, the cartel soon broke down. At this time, the Union realized that it was to their advantage not to exchange prisoners. As a result, large prisons such as Andersonville were created. The earliest camps for Union prisoners during the Civil War were in and around Richmond, Virginia, capital of the Confederacy. By 1863, the prisoner population in Richmond had grown to

A contemporary view of Camp Sumter in Andersonville, Georgia. Note the earthworks constructed around the prison camp's perimeter that defended it from threats outward as well as from within. *AdeQ Historical Archives.*

One of the reconstructed entrances of Camp Sumter that led into the prison.

One of the existing earthworks that surrounded Camp Sumter. The largest of these was the "Star Fort," from which the camp's administration ran its offices.

the point that it caused a serious drain on the city's dwindling food supply. Richmond was under constant threat of attack.

Commonly known as Andersonville, the military prison facility was officially named Camp Sumter, in honor of the county in which it was located. Construction of the camp began in early 1864 after the decision had been made to relocate Union prisoners to a more secure location. This decision was made because of the battles taking place near Richmond and as a way to procure a greater food supply. Camp Sumter was only in operation for fourteen months; however, during that time forty-five thousand Union soldiers were imprisoned there, and nearly thirteen thousand died from disease, poor sanitation, malnutrition, overcrowding or exposure.

The prison site initially covered approximately 16½ acres of land, which was enclosed by a 15-foot-high stockade wall. The prison was enlarged in June 1864 to 26½ acres to compensate for overpopulation. The stockade was constructed in the shape of a parallelogram that was 1,620 feet long and 779 feet wide. Approximately 19 feet inside of the stockade wall was the "deadline," which the prisoners were not allowed to cross. If a prisoner stepped over the "deadline," the guards in the "pigeon roosts," which were roughly thirty yards apart, were allowed to shoot him.

Due to the threat of Union raids (Sherman's troops were marching on Atlanta), General John H. Winder ordered the building of defensive earthworks and a middle and outer stockade around the prison. Construction of the earthworks began on July 20, 1864. These earthworks consisted of Star Fort, located southwest of the prison, a redoubt located northwest of the north gate and six redans. Several earthworks surrounded the perimeter of the stockade and were constructed to quell disturbances inside the prison and to guard against Union cavalry attacks. The largest of these was Star Fort. Within this stronghold stood the offices of the post commander and the prison commandant. Fort and headquarters were symbols of power, but the fully enclosed earthworks also reflects the authorities' besieged state of mind. Hampered by supply shortages and a constant influx of new prisoners, Confederates here were responsible for operating a prison camp under conditions they could hardly control. Four of the Star Fort's guns were trained outward to repel Union cavalry raids. The other five cannon were aimed toward the north slope of the prison camp.

The first prisoners arrived at Camp Sumter in February 1864. Over the course of the next few months, approximately four hundred prisoners arrived daily. By June 1864, more than twenty-six thousand prisoners were confined here. The stockade was only designed to house ten thousand. The largest number of prisoners held at one time was thirty-two thousand in August 1864. Due to the deteriorating economy, inadequate transportation and the need to concentrate all resources on its army, the Confederate government was unable to provide the prisoners with adequate housing, food, clothing and medical care, Due to the terrible conditions and breakdown of the prisoner exchange system, prisoners suffered greatly, and a high mortality rate ensued.

On July 9, 1864, Sergeant David Kennedy of the Ninth Ohio Cavalry wrote in his diary: "Wuld [sic] that I was an artist & had the material to paint this camp & all its horrors or the tongue of some eloquent Statesman and had the privleage [sic] of expressing my mind to our hon, rulers at Washington, i [sic] should glorery [sic] to describe this hell on Earth where it takes 7 of its ocupiants [sic] to make a Shadow."

When General William T. Sherman's Union forces occupied Atlanta on September 2, 1864, moving Federal cavalry columns within easy striking distance of Andersonville, Confederates moved most of the prisoners to other camps in South Carolina and coastal Georgia. From then until May 1865, Andersonville was operated on a smaller basis than before.

When the war ended, Captain Henry Wirz, the stockade commander, was arrested and charged with conspiring with high Confederate officials to "impair and injure the health and destroy the lives...of Federal prisoners" and "murder, in violation of the laws of war." Such a conspiracy never existed, but anger and indignation throughout the North over the conditions at Andersonville demanded appeasement. Tried and found guilty by a military tribunal, Wirz was hanged in Washington, D.C., on November 10, 1865. A monument to Wirz, erected by the United Daughters of the Confederacy, stands today in the historic town of Andersonville.

Andersonville Prison ceased operation in May 1865. Most former prisoners returned to their prewar occupations. In July and August 1865, nurse Clara Barton, a detachment of laborers and soldiers and a former prisoner named Dorence Atwater came to Andersonville cemetery to identify and mark the graves of the Union dead. As a prisoner, Atwater was assigned to record the names of deceased Union soldiers. Fearing loss of the death record at war's end, Atwater made his own copy in hopes of notifying the relatives of some twelve thousand dead interred here. Thanks to his list and the Confederates records confiscated at the end of the war, only 460 of the Andersonville graves had to be marked "unknown U.S, soldier."

The prison site reverted to private ownership in 1875. In December 1890, it was purchased by the Georgia Department of the Grand Army of the Republic (GAR), a Union veterans' organization. Unable to finance improvements needed to protect the property, this group sold it for one dollar to the Women's Relief Corps, the national auxiliary of the GAR. The Women's Relief Corps (WRC) made many improvements to the area with the idea of creating a memorial park. Pecan trees were planted to produce nuts for sale to help maintain the site, and states began erecting commemorative monuments, The WRC built the Providence Spring House in 1901 to mark the site where, on August 9, 1864, a spring burst forth during a heavy summer rainstorm—an occurrence many prisoners attributed to divine providence. The fountain bowl in the Spring House was purchased through funds raised by former Andersonville prisoners. In 1910, the WRC donated the prison site to the people of the United States. It was administered by the War Department and its successor, the Department of the Army, until its designation as a national historic site by Congress in October 1970. Since July 1, 1971, the park has been administered by the National Park Service.

FEDERAL FORT

Atop the hill to the east was a fort that protected the river bridge, part of the rail line that enabled Sherman to supply his army during the Atlanta Campaign. The rail line has been moved downstream, but piers in the river mark the site of the bridge in 1864. Troops here passed much time in swimming, hiking, picking berries and playing baseball in the field to the west—doubtless some of the first games in this section. Often the men went out seeking food, and sometimes they were fired upon or captured. There was no major battle in the fort area. The Federal Fort State Historical Marker is located on U.S. 41 at the north bank of the Etowah River (Bartow County).

ATLANTA'S DEFENSES

There are little traces of the Confederate defenses that protected Atlanta during the Civil War. The few seen today are a few entrenchments and Fort Walker. One line of earthworks in Adams Park is one of the few remaining sections of the exterior portion of Atlanta's defenses designed as a barrier to Federal attempts to cut the two railroads that enter the city from the southwest. Built about August 1, it joined the main line of city fortifications at West Fair and Ashby Streets, from which it ran southwest to East Point

Peachtree Street Fort. The Confederate defenses of Atlanta consisted of numerous earthen forts and redoubts such as Fort Walker in Grant Park. *AdeQ Historical Archives.*

Fort Walker as it appears today in Atlanta's Grant Park.

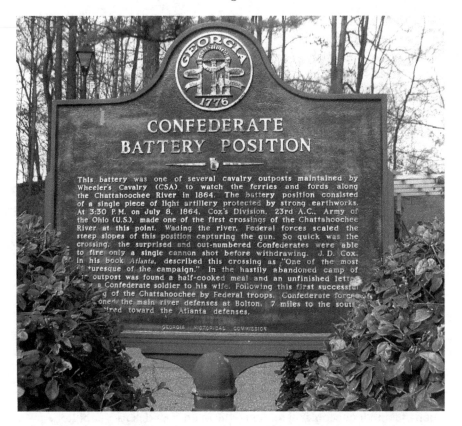

A historical marker marking the location of another of Atlanta's extensive defenses built during the Civil War. The marker is in a cul-de-sac at the end of River Chase Point, off River Chase Circle, which is off Heards Ferry Road in Sandy Springs. *AdeQ Historical Archives.*

(later prolonged to Thames' Mill in Clayton County). Manned by troops of Hardee's and S.D. Lee's corps, it withstood all Federal attempts to seize it and was abandoned only when the Federals cut the railroads at Fairburn and Jonesboro. The 1864 State Historical Marker and preserved earthworks are located in Adams Park (off the end of Mill Acres Drive) in Atlanta (Fulton County).

Fort Walker formed the southeastern salient of Atlanta's inner line of fortifications erected during the summer and fall of 1863. The line consisted of a cordon of redoubts on hills connected by rifle pits encircling the city, aggregating some ten and a half miles of earthworks designed and supervised by Colonel L.P. Grant, pioneer citizen, construction engineer and railroad builder of Atlanta. After almost 150 years, it is one of a few remnants of a line that withstood the quartering steel and climbing fire of Federal armies for forty-two days—evacuated only when the remaining railroad was cut. The fort was named for Major General W.H.T. Walker, who was killed in the Battle of Atlanta. The Fort Walker State Historical Marker is located in front of the preserved fortification in Grant Park, Atlanta, Georgia (Fulton County).

For those fortifications no longer visible, there are a few historical markers marking some of the locations of the Confederate as well as Union earthworks in Atlanta's neighborhoods. The Sandy Springs Confederate Battery is one such location. This battery was one of several cavalry outposts maintained by Wheeler's Cavalry (CSA) to watch the ferries and fords along the Chattahoochee River in 1864. The battery position consisted of a single piece of light artillery protected by strong earthworks. At 3:30 p.m. on July 8, 1864, Cox's Division, Twenty-third Army Corps, Army of the Ohio (U.S.), made one of the first crossings of the Chattahoochee River at this point. Wading the river, Federal forces scaled the steep slopes of this position capturing the gun. So quick was the crossing that the surprised and outnumbered Confederates were able to fire only a single cannon shot before withdrawing. J.D. Cox, in his book *Atlanta*, described this crossing as "one of the most picturesque of the campaign." In the hastily abandoned camp of the outpost was found a half-cooked meal and an unfinished letter from a Confederate soldier to his wife. Following this first successful crossing of the Chattahoochee by Federal troops, Confederate forces abandoned the main river defenses at Bolton, seven miles to the south, and retired toward the Atlanta defenses. The Confederate Battery Position State Historical Marker is located on a cul-de-sac on River Chase Point in Sandy Springs (Fulton County).

Another historical marker marks the site of Sector of Siege Line located on Eighth Street just east of Penn Avenue in Atlanta. Fifty-five yards southeast from the marker was an entrenched line of field works that crossed this block, extending southwest to Seventh Street, where it turned northwest to Juniper at Eleventh Street. This was a sector of the Federal siege line occupied by troops of Brigadier General T.J. Wood's Third Division of Howard's (later Stanley's) Fourth Corps, from July 22 to August 25, 1864 (with these dates representing the period of siege operations). Lieutenant Ambrose G. Bierce, topographical officer of Hazen's brigade, Wood's division, was later known as an author of stories relating to his experiences in the Federal army— perhaps the only instance of literary attainment deriving there from the campaign for Atlanta.

While this line of fortification no longer exists, a marker tells of how hard fought these positions were between the Confederate and Federal forces. On July 22, 1864, Light Battery H, First Illinois (with four twenty-pounders), under Captain Francis DeGress, was posted here on the right of M.L. Smith's division, Logan's Fifteenth Army Corps. Shells from these guns are said to have been the first to fall in Atlanta. In late afternoon. Manigault's brigade (Confederate) broke the Federal line at the railroad, forcing Martin's brigade south of it and Lightburn's north of it to withdraw. DeGress's gunners spiked the pieces, and the horses were shot to prevent the removal of the guns by their Confederate captors. The line was retaken in a countercharge by Martin and Lightburn, aided by Mersy's Sixteenth AC brigade. Captain DeGress repossessed his guns. The DeGress Battery State Historical Marker is located on DeGress Avenue (where it turns east) north of DeKalb Avenue in Atlanta.

The Exterior Line State Historical Marker, located at Cascade Avenue and Martin Luther King Drive in Atlanta, marked the extant of the exterior line of defenses of Atlanta during July–August 1864. When Federal forces east of Atlanta were shifted to the west side, to move against the Macon and the West Point railroads (entering the city from the southwest), the Confederate defenders entrenched a line west of a parallel to them. This line began at West Fair and Ashby Streets and ran west to and beyond this point, ending at the Georgia Military Academy in College Park. Siege operations (July 28–August 25) were barren of results and ceased with transfer of Federal forces south to Fairburn and Jonesboro, where the seizure of the railroads and the consequent evacuation of Atlanta ended the campaign.

CAMP LAWTON

Camp Lawton was hastily constructed in the late summer and fall of 1864 to alleviate the horrendous overcrowding and supply and health problems of the Confederate military prison at Andersonville (Camp Sumter), Georgia, that eventually resulted in the deaths of nearly thirteen thousand Union POWs. Located along the Augusta and Savannah Railroad five miles north of what was then Millen Junction in Burke County, the new prison facility was modeled after Camp Sumter but, in its execution and operation, was an improvement in most respects.

Situated in a shallow valley through which flowed a spring-fed stream, the prison featured a forty-two-acre compound framed by a fifteen-foot-high stockade wall of locally harvested pine logs. At regular intervals along the outside walls, guards were stationed in "pigeon roosts" to keep watch over the inmates. A low fence of pine scantlings ran thirty feet inside the perimeter of the stockade wall and served as a "dead line" to keep prisoners away from the wall. Several brick ovens equipped with kettles were built for cooking purposes, although prisoners typically cooked their rations individually and in small messes. The stream flowed through the prison, bisecting it. The upstream portion was used for washing and drinking, and the downstream portion served as a latrine. A wooden bridge crossed the stream at the point where a sutler's cabin stood. Ancillary facilities—at least three earthworks, a guards' camp and hospital, log buildings for administrative purposes, a POW hospital and two burial grounds for POWs—were located around the stockade.

The prison guard was possibly composed of elements of the First, Second, Third and Fourth Georgia Reserves, the Florida Light Artillery and the Fifty-fifth Georgia. Commanded by Colonel Henry Forno, the reserve units were composed basically of teenage males and older men who were poorly equipped and trained. The prison commandant was Captain D.W. Vowles, and the chief surgeon was Dr. Isaiah H. White. On November 8, Vowles submitted the only existent camp return to the Richmond authorities. It listed 10,299 POWs at the prison, of whom 349 had enlisted in the Confederate army, 486 had died and 285 were working at the prison. In addition, the commissary general of prisons in Alabama and Georgia, General John H. Winder, established his headquarters there. Moreover, just before the prison was evacuated, Winder was promoted to commissary general of prisons east of the Mississippi. Therefore, for a time the administrative apparatus of much of the Confederate military prisons was located at Camp Lawton.

Living conditions in a Civil War prison were harsh. Those Federal veteran POWs who had been moved from Andersonville Prison did not fare any better in Camp Lawton. The South's dwindling resources and inability to manage a prisoner of war population where disease and poor sanitation were in abundance began to take hold. "The weather has been rainy and cold at nights," Private Robert Knox Sneden, who was previously imprisoned at Andersonville, wrote in his diary on November 1, 1864. "Many prisoners have died from exposure, as not more than half of us have any shelter but a blanket propped upon sticks…Our rations have grown smaller in bulk too, and we have the same hunger as of old."

The impending arrival of Federal forces during Sherman's March to the Sea soon forced the Confederates to move the prisoners elsewhere, including Florence, South Carolina, Savannah and Blackshear. The camp was abandoned between November 17 and 22, nearly six weeks after the first prisoners have arrived. In early December 1864, Union cavalry found the empty prison, a freshly dug area and a board reading "650 buried here." Outraged, troops apparently burned much of the stockade and the camp buildings and a depot and a hotel in Millen, which was a transportation hub.

In fact, about 725 Union soldiers died at Camp Lawton. Following the war, the army quartermaster general's office consolidated the burials of Union dead and established the short-lived Lawton National Cemetery on a four-acre plot near the site of the former prison. A dispute with the landowner led to the closure of the cemetery in February 1868, and the bodies were transferred to Beaufort (South Carolina) National Cemetery.

Today, little remains of the prison stockade; however, the earthen breastworks that guarded it may still be seen. During 2010, Georgia Southern University archaeology teams uncovered the stockade wall and numerous personal articles from the soldiers imprisoned there. The site is part of the Magnolia Springs State Park near Millen.

Blackshear Confederate Prison Camp

A historical marker stands on the site of a Confederate prison camp for Union prisoners of war. Established about November 18, 1864, the camp held more than five thousand prisoners until the first week of January 1865. These prisoners were brought here from Camp Lawton near Millen and probably from Andersonville to avoid the possibility of their being liberated by Sherman's troops, who were then moving southward. The camp was at one time under the command of Colonel H. Forno. Other prisoners from Millen were transferred to camps at Savannah and Florence. The Confederate Prison Camp State Historical Marker is located on Georgia 203 just north of Blackshear, Georgia (Pierce County).

Fort Tyler

At the crest of the hill stood Fort Tyler, the last Confederate fort to fall in the War Between the States. Fort Tyler was of earthwork construction, thirty-five yards square surrounded by a ditch twelve feet wide and ten feet deep and enclosed by wooden abates. The fort was erected to protect important railroad and wagon bridges across the Chattahoochee River east of this point.

Fort Tyler was a square earthwork fortification built atop a high hill in West Point, and its primary purpose was to defend the vital bridge over

Fort Tyler in West Point became one of the last battles fought east of the Mississippi in the Civil War.

the Chattahoochee River at West Point, a city uniquely located on the west side of the river on a point of land formed by the Alabama border and the Chattahoochee. Fort Tyler was armed with three pieces of artillery consisting of two field guns and a thirty-two-pounder.

Life at the fort was relatively quiet during the war until the spring of 1865, when Union general James Wilson began his devastating raid across Alabama and Georgia. Dividing his advancing force, Wilson moved with one column against Columbus to the south, while Colonel Oscar H. LaGrange led the other column (Second and Fourth Indiana, Seventh Kentucky and First Wisconsin) against West Point and Fort Tyler. Battles for both Columbus and West Point took place on April 16, 1865, an Easter Sunday. Although neither side knew it at the time, General Robert E. Lee had surrendered the Army of Northern Virginia a full seven days earlier.

When LaGrange arrived at West Point, he found Fort Tyler occupied by roughly between 120 and 265 Confederates led by Brigadier General Robert C. Tyler. Wounded repeatedly during the war, he had lost a leg at Missionary Ridge. His little garrison was a mixture of regulars, convalescents, militia and volunteers. In fact, the garrison contained remnants of Point Coupe Louisiana and Waittes' South Carolina Batteries. Tyler's command consisted of the following officers: Colonel J.H. Fannin; Captains Gonzales, Trepanier and Webb; and Lieutenants Montgomery and McFarland.

Flying a Confederate battle flag presented to him by the citizens of West Point, the general defended Fort Tyler with a vicious tenacity. Using his limited artillery and volleys of musket fire, Tyler held back three Federal regiments of approximately 3,500 men sent by LaGrange to attack the fort for most of the day. Both sides exchanged fierce artillery fire in an encounter that became known as the Battle of West Point. Local lore held that prior to the battle General Tyler had promised that he would either achieve victory or die in the effort. He died while walking in front of the wall of the fort in a gesture of defiance to the attacking Federals. When the battle finally ended, Fort Tyler surrendered. Union casualties included 7 killed and 29 wounded. Confederate losses were 19 killed, 28 wounded and 218 missing (captured). The dead, including General Tyler, from the battle were buried across the river at the Fort Tyler Cemetery. The stone home of Dr. A.W. Griggs, Confederate surgeon, built in 1858, stands forty feet northwest. Although hit repeatedly by cannon fire of both forces, its original walls are intact. Here Mrs. Griggs and other West Point women gave aid and shelter to wounded of both armies after battle.

A historical marker is at the intersection of West Tenth Street and Sixth Avenue in West Point, Georgia (Troup County). A beautifully reconstructed Fort Tyler can be found on its original site, which was reclaimed after years of use as a city reservoir. The fort is located on Sixth Avenue, half a block north of Tenth Street near downtown West Point.

Chapter 4
MODERN GEORGIA, 1866–2011

FORT MCPHERSON

The history of the army in Atlanta has evolved from the state militia's use of a pasture—where Fort McPherson sits today—for a meeting place and drill ground in 1835 to the current army presence at Fort McPherson, Fort Gillem and various locations throughout Atlanta.

With anticipation of the Civil War, the old muster grounds at Fort McPherson in southwest Atlanta became a training ground for troops. After the Acts of Secession, the Confederate government took active charge of the old parade ground, erected barracks and established a cartridge factory to supply the Southern troops in this district. The Confederate troops destroyed the cartridge factory and many of the barracks during the siege of Atlanta and the eventual evacuation of the city.

Following the Civil War, thirty-seven Georgia counties, including the city of Atlanta, were organized into the District of Allatoona, with headquarters in Marietta. Atlanta eventually became the headquarters of the Third Military District of the military reconstruction of Georgia. The last commander was General George G. Meade, who remained in command until July 30, 1868, when civil authority was restored.

From 1867 to 1868, a ten-company post was constructed on the fifty-three acres of leased ground at the southwest corner of Atlanta, and on December 30, 1867, it was named McPherson Barracks in honor of Union major general James Birdseye McPherson, U.S. Volunteers (brigadier general, USA). He was killed July 22, 1864, during the Battle of Atlanta.

Main entrance to Fort McPherson as it appeared during the First World War. *AdeQ Historical Archives.*

During World War I, another military facility, Camp Jesup, was built next to Fort McPherson. Constructed by local civilians and German prisoners of war, Jesup served as a major center for repairing, overhauling and reconstructing vehicles and as a storage area for transport supplies. Jesup's facilities included living quarters, mess halls and administrative buildings. During the peak of war activity, nearly 4,000 civilian and 2,100 military personnel were employed at the camp. Jesup remained active after the war as a motor transport school, a general depot and a quartermaster intermediate storage depot. Camp Jesup was deactivated on August 23, 1927. This building is simply identified as "Y" No. 7. *AdeQ Historical Archives.*

"Retreat" at Fort McPherson during World War II. *AdeQ Historical Archives.*

Between the years 1867 and 1881, the barracks was garrisoned in turn by elements of the Second, Sixteenth and Eighteenth U.S. Infantry regiments and the Fifth Artillery. Their mission was to enforce Union regulations during the Reconstruction period following the Civil War.

In October 1881, Secretary of War Robert T. Lincoln directed that the lease of the site be surrendered and the buildings sold at public auction. In compliance with this directive, McPherson Barracks was abandoned by United States troops on December 8, 1881. The U.S. Treasury realized $17,264.40 from the sale of the buildings.

During the period from 1881 to 1886, McPherson Barracks continued to serve as a summer encampment due to its climate, especially for troops assigned to subtropical Florida. Congress, aware of the location's popularity, authorized the establishment of a permanent military post in the area.

On March 3, 1885, Congress passed the Sundry Civil Bill, which contained an initial sum of $15,000 for the purchase of land and erection of a ten-company post. The task of site selection went to Major General Winfield Scott Hancock, commanding general of the Division of the Atlantic. Five tracts of land amounting to 14,009 acres were purchased in September 1885. Captain Joshua W. Jacobs, assistant quartermaster, was totally responsible for developing and implementing the first master plan for the post. In August 1886, Congress authorized the purchase of an adjoining

96.31 acres. The original boundaries of the new post contained just over 26 acres of land. The magnitude of Jacob's undertaking can be appreciated when it is considered that he had to build a small self-contained community from vacant woodland. Today, forty of the original buildings are listed on the National Register of Historic Places and, as such, are preserved and protected as important elements of national heritage.

During World War I, Fort McPherson was used as a camp for Imperial German navy prisoners of war. During the general textile workers strike in 1934, this fort was used as a detention center to hold picketers who had been arrested while striking at a Newnan, Georgia cotton mill.

Fort McPherson's nearest army neighbor, and its subpost, is Fort Gillem, which is located in Forest Park, Georgia, not too far away. Fort Gillem is a logistical support base, housing some army, Department of Defense and other government agencies. Those units include the First Army, the U.S. Army and Air Force Exchange Distribution Center, the Military Entrance Processing Station and the U.S. Army Second Recruiting Brigade. Fort Gillem also hosts the only crime lab of the U.S. Army. Fort McPherson and Fort Gillem share most common services.

In 2007, there were 2,453 active duty soldiers and 3,784 civilian employees at both forts, with a total active duty and civilian employee payroll of $529,874,972. With only 102 family quarters and 272 single soldier billets at Fort McPherson, and 10 family quarters at Fort Gillem, the active duty military and Department of the Army civilian employees live in civilian housing in the surrounding Fulton, DeKalb, Clayton, Fayette and Henry Counties.

As a result of the 2005 BRAC commission recommendation, Fort McPherson is scheduled to be closed down and Fort Gillem to be reduced to a military enclave as of September 15, 2011. The following units are scheduled to relocate from Fort McPherson: the Headquarters of the U.S. Army Forces Command and the Headquarters of the U.S. Army Reserve Command will be moved to Fort Bragg, North Carolina; the Headquarters of U.S. Army Central will be moved to Shaw Air Force Base, South Carolina; the Installation Management Command, Southeast Region, and the U.S. Army Network Enterprise Technology Command, Southeastern Region, will be moved to Fort Eustis, Virginia; and the Army Contracting Agency, Southern Region Office, will be moved to Fort Sam Houston, Texas.

Fort Screven

The legislature of Georgia in 1786 passed a law providing for a fort on Cockspur or Tybee Island to be named in honor of General James Screven, Revolutionary War hero. It was never built by the state. In 1808, the federal government obtained jurisdiction over the property on Tybee Island now known as Fort Screven Reservation. The actual title was acquired in 1875, and the post, established in 1898, was in continuous use from the Spanish-American War through both World Wars. Primarily a coast artillery fort, at one time Fort Fremont in South Carolina was under its jurisdiction. It

A postcard showing life at Fort Screven during the First World War. *AdeQ Historical Archives.*

In 1961, Battery Garland, the former gun battery and magazine for a twelve-inch long-range gun, became the Tybee Island museum. Rooms that once stored six-hundred-pound projectiles and two-hundred-pound bags of gunpowder now hold the collections and exhibits of over four hundred years of the history Tybee Island and Fort Screven.

Fort Screven's Battery Backus once had a 6.00-inch Armstrong and two 4.72-inch Armstrong guns as part of its armament. This how the battery appeared in 2008.

A few of the batteries of Fort Screven remain preserved through odd means, such this battery serving as a base for a home.

Cockspur Island saw one more military use after the War Between the States. During the Spanish-American War, a small force was garrisoned there to protect the river mouth. The army operated the controls for electric mines in the Savannah River, manned guns in Fort Pulaski's demilune and constructed Battery Hambright in 1899. The battery held two emplacements for three-inch rapid-fire guns.

Various styles of military architecture can be found throughout Georgia and in the American South. Seen here is the armory for the Savannah Volunteer Guards. The Savannah Volunteer Guards were formed in 1802. This armory was erected in 1892. Since 1979, the Savannah Volunteer Guards Armory has been part of the Savannah College Art & Design. *AdeQ Historical Archives*.

This armory building for the Georgia Hussars was located on 3 Liberty Street in Savannah, and since 1923 it has been home to the Knights of Columbus Council 631.

In Savannah's Forsyth Park are two concrete "dummy forts" that are fashioned after the Endicott-era Coast Artillery batteries. These were in use by the Savannah Volunteer Guard as training aids. In 1901, by an act of the Georgia legislature, the Savannah Volunteer Guards become designated as "heavy artillery" and shortly thereafter the "Coast Artillery Corps, National Guard, Georgia." At the outbreak of the First World War, they were mustered into the U.S. Army under the command of Major G. Heyward and served as the Sixty-first Coast Artillery Company, Expeditionary Force, in France, as tractor-drawn army artillery.

View of the other "dummy fort" in Forsyth Park, Savannah. These were built around 1910 and are known by locals as East and West Dummy Forts.

became an infantry post and finally a school for deep-sea diving. Many distinguished officers saw duty here, including General George C. Marshall as colonel in command. In 1945, Fort Screven was declared surplus by the War Department and acquired by the town of Savannah Beach. The Tybee Island State Historical Marker is located at the Tybee Museum across the street from the Tybee Island Lighthouse (Chatham County).

Camp Thomas

In 1895, Congress established the Chickamauga National Military Park to preserve the land and honor those who had fought and died there. Anticipating military needs to house thousands for training, Congress legislated in May 1896 that the army could use all military parks with their vast acreage as training grounds. In 1898, Camp Thomas, named for General George H. Thomas, the "Rock of Chickamauga," was created to meet the needs of the Spanish-American War. Over seven thousand regular army infantry, cavalry and artillery units were stationed here from April 14 to May 14 and then embarked for service in Cuba via the Western and Atlantic and the Chattanooga, Rome and Southern Railroads. The next day, more than fifty-eight thousand men and ten to fifteen thousand horses of the First, Third and Sixth Volunteer Corps arrived. The park provided the space, available water, railroads, climate and terrain to house the men and horses, to acclimate them to the hot climate they would meet in the Caribbean and to practice on terrain both hilly (Snodgrass Hill area) and flat (Brock Field area). The volunteers then shipped out to Puerto Rico. Camp Thomas began closing in August 1898, and it took years for the battlefield to recover. In the wake of the war, the army concluded that permanent posts were necessary.

Fort Oglethorpe

The site of Fort Oglethorpe was selected by a board of officers in August 1902 and is situated on lands acquired by the Chickamauga Park Commission under the provisions of an act of Congress. The new reservation was first known as Chickamauga Park (New Post). The post was located entirely within the limits of the Chickamauga and Chattanooga National Military Park in Catoosa and Walker Counties. The total area of the park was

Fort Oglethorpe began life as a cavalry post in the early part of the twentieth century. *AdeQ Historical Archives.*

During World War II, Fort Oglethorpe became a major training facility for the Women's Army Corps (WAC). *AdeQ Historical Archives.*

Fort Oglethorpe's parade ground still bears traces of a cavalry post, as evidenced by these cavalry horse training obstacles and the row of officers' homes in the distance.

approximately 6,541.64 acres, of which the military post composed an area of about 813.42 acres.

The permanent post was named Fort Oglethorpe in 1902 and substantially completed by 1904. Various cavalry regiments were stationed at the post, and although tents and barracks were removed from the old Camp Thomas, the battlefield was still used for maneuvers. However, various states, Congress and historical societies continued with their plans to restore the battlefield to its general appearance of 1863.

A great blow came to the Chickamauga-Chattanooga Park during World War I, when Fort Oglethorpe was expanded to the south on the park grounds. Three contiguous camps were enjoying separate existences in the area. These, however, were incorporated, making the southern expansion necessary. During the war, troops marched en masse in the streets. Wooden barracks grew up among the monuments on the battlefield, and on the post ground, polo teams vied in the polo grounds on Barnhardt Circle and trenches and war games spun across the nearby countryside. By 1918, more than 1,600 post buildings were on the expanded Fort Oglethorpe and more than sixty thousand troops had been mobilized through the post.

Around Barnhardt Circle were the detention camps for the German prisoners of war and enemy aliens. To the west was the post hospital, site of the present Tri-County Memorial Facility. On the Camp Greenleaf site, one of the camps that merged into the Fort Oglethorpe Post, the army established a medical and sanitary corp. Many of the horse-drawn ambulances that crossed the war's battlefields had their origin at Fort Oglethorpe, where the formation and training was a Camp Greenleaf specialty. Furthermore, the sanitary procedures prescribed for trench warfare and trench life also arose in the Sanitary Corps' method of development at Fort Oglethorpe. The post became temporarily a home for a number of cavalry regiments, notably the Third, Sixth, Seventh, Tenth, Eleventh and Twelfth. The Sixth Cavalry was frequently stationed at the post, and by July 4, 1919, the War Department had resolved to make Fort Oglethorpe the permanent post and home of the Sixth Cavalry. This unit remained at Fort Oglethorpe until 1942.

The end of the First World War saw a reduction in the number of wooden barracks and tent camps on the Chickamauga battlefield portion of Fort Oglethorpe. As with all military posts after the war, things began to slow down at Fort Oglethorpe between 1918 and 1940. The Sixth Cavalry continued their maneuvers in the area, and polo was a popular sport. Barnhardt Circle saw many matches, mock war games, horseshows, parades and other military forms of recreation.

By 1941, mechanization was approaching rapidly, and Fort Oglethorpe saw the addition of bantam cars to the post. Although horses were retained for a short time after, in 1942, with the transfer of the Sixth Cavalry to South Carolina and the horses gone, the vehicular unit had grown to five hundred. World War II saw the enlargement of Fort Oglethorpe. An induction center was established, and many residents of the greater Chattanooga area can recall their induction into army life at Fort Oglethorpe. Prison barracks and stockades again grew on the post, and prisoners of war and enemy aliens again sat out the war at Fort Oglethorpe. The largest of these stockades was situated only a stone's throw from today's city hall.

Around Barnhardt Circle, barracks were re-erected. At first these housed a provost marshal school, but later the MPs relocated to another barracks in what is now downtown Fort Oglethorpe. This new barracks was later turned into the Women's Third Army Corps Training Center in 1943. By September 1943, all men had been removed from the post, and five thousand women were undergoing training. The men's induction center still remained.

In 1943, President Roosevelt visited the post to inspect the women's training program. In July 1945, the WAC center was closed down, and the post was turned into a redistribution center for processing the thousands of GIs receiving their discharge.

In December 1946, the end of an era struck Fort Oglethorpe. It was decided to permanently retire the post, and by 1947, the entire establishment was declared surplus. By January 1948, the War Assets Administration had sold most of the old post on the open market. Many interested civilians and civilian neighbors of the post took advantage of the sale to attempt a novel approach in municipal administration: the creation of a ready-made town.

Over one hundred buildings of the old post remained, many dating back to 1904 and many remaining serviceable for use as residences and business sites. The sale of lands to the north and east of the post offered prepared home sites for suburban developments, with water, sewerage and electricity remaining from the post days. The attempt to create a growing community on the old post facility and keeping memories of the old post was a success, and in March 1949, the civilian city of Fort Oglethorpe was formally incorporated, the first town to receive articles of incorporation in Georgia in twenty-five years. A museum dedicated to the history of the military post and of the Sixth United States Cavalry Regiment currently exists on the former parade ground of the military post.

CAMP WHEELER

During World War I, the city fathers in Macon wanted an army camp located here. To that end, they enlisted the aid of Harry Stillwell Edwards, the famous local author and poet. After agreeing to help, Edwards traveled to New York in an attempt to meet with General Leonard Wood, who was in charge of the selection process at that time. Edwards enlisted the aid of his friend Teddy Roosevelt, who wrote a note of introduction on a personal calling card. General Leonard Wood came to Macon in May 1917 to make a final choice. The 21,480-acre site chosen included Holly Bluff, the home of Harry Stillwell Edwards and formerly the plantation of Colonel Andrew Jackson Lane, CSA, father of Mrs. Edwards.

The camp was named for Joseph Wheeler, who was born in Augusta, Georgia. Wheeler, an 1859 West Point graduate, had the distinction of serving as a lieutenant general in the Confederate army. It was established on July 18, 1917, as a temporary training camp for National Guard units in

Camp Wheeler's regimental street during the First World War. *AdeQ Historical Archives.*

Camp Wheeler as it appeared during World War II. *AdeQ Historical Archives.*

federal service and consisted primarily of tents in a cantonment area. Major General F.J. Kernan became the first camp commander in August 1917, and troop strength reached a high point of 28,960 in July 1918. A cavalry remount depot was at nearby Mogul, and a range was at Phillips Station. In

December 1918, the camp was ordered closed. The military officially closed the first Camp Wheeler on April 10, 1919.

In 1940, prudence dictated that America increase its military training. Accordingly, in October 1940, Congressman Carl Vinson's office announced that Camp Wheeler would be rebuilt and was scheduled to be ready for operation by March 15, 1941. The base was reestablished on October 8, 1940, with construction beginning on December 21, 1940. Rather than being used to train entire units, the camp was an infantry replacement training center where new recruits received basic and advanced individual training to replace combat casualties. The camp was divided into three major portions: a cantonment area, a maneuver area and a main impact area. At the height of the training effort, the camp contained seventeen thousand trainees and three thousand cadre personnel.

The camp's first commander was Colonel A.R. Emery, for whom Emery Highway was later named. Although nearly one-third smaller in area (14,394 acres) than the World War I facility, the construction was to be far more substantial. Where wooden floors and tents had been the order of the day during the First World War, steel-reinforced concrete foundations topped with wooden buildings were the new standards. The total cost of construction was reported to be $13,550,485.

The camp had a housing capacity for about 24,603 enlisted men and 1,290 officers. Many of the men who worked on the huge Great Depression–era archaeological projects at nearby Ocmulgee National Monument were reassigned to Camp Wheeler. Construction eventually included facilities to house approximately 2,000 prisoners of war. There were also twenty-four branch camps for the POWs in Georgia, with eight of those located in the central Georgia area under the auspices of Camp Wheeler. At one time, the number of prisoners stationed at the Wheeler Camp and its branch camps was about 4,700. At the height of the operation, there were regular Wheeler branch camps at Monticello, Ashburn, Waynesboro, Daniels Field and Dublin. Seasonal work camps were established at Griffin, Sandersville, Fitzgerald and Hawkinsville. Some prisoners worked as mechanics, typewriter experts and tailors, but most worked as laborers in the sawmill or farm areas. They accrued wages at a rate of about eighty cents per day.

As an infantry replacement center, troops were to be trained in virtually all types of small arms used by the military at the time. On December 15, 1945, the last graduation parade was held, with Private Edward A. Winarski of Baltimore, Maryland, being the last graduate. The camp was officially closed on January 19, 1946. Following a decontamination operation in the fall of 1946, the land was returned to the owners.

Additional decontamination operations were completed in 1947 and 1949 to remove munitions and explosives of concern (MEC) from the site. After the decontamination operations, more MEC was discovered at the site. At this time, the South Atlantic Division of the U.S. Army Corps of Engineers (USACE) instituted a policy that provided for an annual visual inspection of the camp. While this policy was in place, until 1966, MEC was regularly found each year of the inspection. During this time, several landowners of the former camp area sued the United States for the depreciation of the property value as a result of the kaolin deposits due to the presence of MEC. In nine of these cases, the owners received monetary consideration.

The whole area is now an industrial park, but there are lots of open areas that look like they might have once been training grounds.

DUBLIN TEMPORARY PRISONER OF WAR CAMP

As the United States became more involved in World War II, more farm products were needed in support of the war effort. The problem was that many of the farmers were no longer fighting the weather but were instead fighting in Europe and the Pacific. Those at home aided the war effort by stepping up agricultural production. In 1943, State Senator Herschel Lovett, County Agent Harry Edge and Emergency Farm Labor Assistant Walter B. Daniel contacted Congressman Carl Vinson of Milledgeville to request the location of a temporary prisoner of war camp in Dublin.

Laurens County needed help in gathering the crops that would be ready for harvest in the summer through early fall. The gentlemen requested that a camp be set up at the county farm on Highway 441 just above the present interstate highway. Vinson contacted Colonel I.B. Summers of the Prisoner of War Division of the federal government. Colonel Summers advised Vinson that the location of the camp would not be easy because of the lack of trained prison guards. Vinson, undaunted, contacted Colonel R.E. Patterson of the prison camp at Camp Wheeler, near Macon. Colonel Patterson echoed the doubts about a camp for Dublin.

Under the guidelines of the Geneva Convention of 1929, prisoners of war must be paid eighty cents per day for labor outside of the prison camp. Prison labor was limited by the number of guards, not the number of prisoners. The Farm Labor Advisory Committee—consisting of Bob Hodges, Wade Dominy, C.L. Thigpen, R.T. Gilder, H.W. Ozier, Frank Clark, D.W. Alligood and A.O. Hadden—continued to press Vinson to acquire the camp to help in the harvest. Finally, Vinson succeeded, and the army allowed some prisoners to be sent from Camp Wheeler.

The first couple hundred prisoners arrived on August 26, 1943, under the supervision of Captain Henry J. Bordeaux. The first prisoners were Italians. The camp was not located on the county farm but on the site of the old Twelfth District Fairgrounds. The fairgrounds were bounded on the north by the railroad east by Troup Street, south by Telfair Street and west by Joiner Street. The prisoners arrived just in time to help with the peanut harvesting in Laurens and surrounding counties. The camp was completed in three days under the U.S. Army Corps of Engineers and the Quartermaster Corps. After the camp was set up, the prisoners were immediately taken to the fields. The men were used to chop cotton and stack peanuts.

By October, the need for farm labor had significantly declined. The army planned to move the camp by mid- October. The Fourth Service Command granted permission for the camp to remain open into November. Half of the five hundred prisoners were moved in the third week of October, along with their guards, under the leadership of Captain Jennings. New guards were brought in to replace those who left. Shortly, the camp would close down for the winter.

Camp Hancock, near Augusta, as it appeared during the First World War. It was established on July 18, 1917, as a training camp for National Guard troops. The post was designated as a demobilization center on December 3, 1918, and ordered salvaged January 2, 1919. A caretaker detachment took possession after the post had been abandoned on March 27, 1919. *AdeQ Historical Archives*.

Just as the Allied forces began the invasion of Europe in June 1944, the German prisoners returned to Dublin. It would be a long, hot summer for the German prisoners in Dublin. One prisoner was killed by a falling tree on Snellgrove plantation. On July Fourth, three prisoners—Josef Damer, Jeorge Fries and Willi Pape—escaped while on a work detail at the Warner Callan Farm near Scott. They were captured the following day. The commandant of the camp, not believing that the POWs got lost in the woods, instituted harsh disciplinary procedures as a result of the escape. The prisoners countered by staging a sit-down strike and refusing to work on the farms. Within a few days, calmer heads prevailed. The matter was settled. By the end of the summer, the situation had eased, and the army guards had enough free time to play baseball, basketball and football games against the U.S. Navy at the new naval hospital built nearby.

The prisoners were sent the following summer to help the farmers in harvesting their crops, which were still needed for the war effort. With the end of the war in August 1945, there was no longer a need for the camp. The camp closed in early January 1946. As of 2011, one lone barracks from the camp still stands at the corner of Troup Street and the railroad tracks.

CAMP GORDON

Constructed during America's rush to mobilize for World War I, Camp Gordon was one of sixteen temporary training camps, the largest in the southern states and the focus of Atlanta's wartime patriotic spirit. It served as the birthplace and training ground for the legendary Eighty-second "All American" division and based hospital No. 43, the Emory University Medical Unit.

Built under the supervision of Major J.N. Pease, QM Corps, and engineered by Lockwood-Greene & Co., Camp Gordon was the largest construction project in Atlanta history to that time. Ready for troop occupancy in just five months, the camp's 2,400 acres included 1,635 buildings with barracks for 46,612 men and corral space for 7,688 horses and mules. The November 11, 1918 armistice ended the Great War and the need for Camp Gordon. It was salvaged and abandoned by 1921.

The Emory Unit served in France and was reactivated for World War II. Atlanta's own Eighty-second Division fought with distinction in the St. Mihiel and Meuse-Argonne offensives, suffered 8,077 casualties and produced the most decorated hero of the war, Sergeant Alvin York. It was

Soldiers receiving instruction in Camp Gordon, near Atlanta, during the First World War. *AdeQ Historical Archives.*

reactivated for World War II as the Eighty-second Airborne Division. The Camp Gordon State Historical Marker is located inside the main entrance to DeKalb-Peachtree Airport near the intersection of Airport and Clairmont Roads (DeKalb County).

Fort Benning

Outgrowing the limited ranges at the Presidio in Monterey, California, the School of Musketry co-located with the School of Fire at Fort Sill, Oklahoma, in 1913. Both schools languished within a few years as both instructors and students were needed to secure the border with civil war–torn Mexico and for the punitive expedition of 1916. Upon the declaration of war with the Central Powers on April 6, 1917, it became apparent that the infantry, field artillery and the Thirty-fifth Division could not continue to train on the same ranges at Fort Sill. The War Department needed dozens of new facilities to muster and train the millions of Doughboys required in Europe as soon as possible. By the summer of 1918, the infantry was casting about for a new home.

In an attempt to lure an army training camp to the Columbus area, the Encampment Committee of the Chamber of Commerce of Columbus,

Infantry barracks in Fort Benning as it appeared during the 1930s. *AdeQ Historical Archives.*

Aerial view of Fort Benning in the 1980s. *AdeQ Historical Archives.*

Georgia, presented a "Proposal for the Lease of Land to the U.S. Government for Establishment of School of Musketry" on January 17, 1918, to representatives of the U.S. Army. Included in the original proposal are endorsements from the Muscogee County commissioners to build access

A reconstructed World War II company street using buildings from various areas of Fort Benning and assembled near the National Infantry Museum.

roads and the Columbus Power Company to build electrical transmission lines if the government accepted the property for a training camp. With options secured on 7,400 of the 9,000 acres proposed at $2 per acre, total estimated construction costs for the cantonment came to $706,000. A formal plan dated January 23 lists a total of 2,008 students, instructors and permanent party to be housed and headquartered in sixty-seven buildings. While the original proposal for the camp envisioned a lease on the land, the army decided later to convert the cantonment to a permanent facility and continue training there after World War I.

On August 17, 1918, a telegram arrived in Columbus confirming the selection of the area for the new site of the army's Infantry School of Arms. By October 6, troops transferring from Fort Sill, Oklahoma, stepped off the train. They stood in formation on October 19, christening the new post Camp Benning in honor of a local Confederate general, Henry Lewis Benning. Unlike most temporary training facilities created in haste during the Great War, Camp Benning survived postwar budget cuts to become a permanent infantry school in 1920. In 1921, the army formally designated the post as the infantry school and changed the name to Fort Benning in 1923.

During the 1920–21 school year, the new school graduated hundreds of lieutenants and captains from the active, reserve and national guard components. In addition to instructors, Camp Benning included demonstration units to support training, an Army Air Corps detachment, the Thirty-second Balloon Observation Company at Lawson Field and the infantry tank school. While the tank school moved to Camp Meade, Maryland, within a year, the infantry tanks moved back to Fort Benning in 1932. In addition to training leaders, Fort Benning became an important center for testing weapons and tactics, publishing professional journals and manuals and developing maneuver doctrine—roles it continues into the twenty-first century. As the home of the largest branch of the army, Fort Benning continued to grow in facilities and troops assigned through the lean years of the Great Depression.

From 1927 to 1932, Lieutenant Colonel George Marshall served as the assistant commandant of the infantry school. In this role, Marshall instituted a rigorous training program known as the "Benning Revolution," preparing thousands of officers for higher command in World War II. The infantry tank units grew through the 1930s until Colonel George S. Patton Jr. and others formed and trained the Second Armored Division at Fort Benning before deploying overseas for combat in World War II. Numerous divisions and smaller units were either federalized or created at Fort Benning during peacetime draft buildup in 1940 and throughout World War II.

In 1940, the airborne "test platoon" initiated the airborne school, which still graduates thousands of parachutists for the United States military each year. The officers' candidate school (OCS) began graduating infantry lieutenants in 1941 and now operates as the only OCS program in the army. More than 100,000 soldiers entered the army as privates or lieutenants at Fort Benning during World War II, and the post earned the nickname the "Benning School for Boys." At the end of the Second World War, Fort Benning remained a vibrant facility as ranger training began. The infantry developed a mechanized component and prepared troops and leaders for the Korean War, Vietnam and other cold war commitments. To date, the U.S. Army Infantry School and Fort Benning have more troops assigned as cadre or in training than any other facility in the United States military.

From 1945 to 1965, Fort Benning transformed to its standard role as an education, testing and doctrine development center. While recruit and officer training increased during the Korean War, from 1950 to 1953, the next major expansion took place during the Vietnam War. The concept of helicopter-borne air assault was tested at Fort Benning for two years before the Eleventh Airborne (Test) Division became the First (Air Assault) Cavalry Division prior to deployment to Vietnam in 1965. Fort Benning was the site of the scout dog school of the United States during the Vietnam War, where the dogs trained to detect ambushes in enemy terrain got their initial training before being transferred to Vietnam for further advanced courses. In addition to greatly expanded OCS, the noncommissioned officer candidate course trained thousands of infantry sergeants from 1967 to 1972, forming the basis for the current noncommissioned officer education system. On several occasions since 1965, brigades and smaller units were formed and trained at Fort Benning to deploy around the world to serve as part of NATO, Desert Storm, Operation Enduring Freedom, Operation Iraqi Freedom and various other missions.

In 1984, following the signing of the Panama Canal Treaty, the School of the Americas relocated from Fort Gulick (Panama) to Fort Benning. After criticism concerning human rights violations committed by a number of graduates in Latin America, the school was renamed Western Hemisphere Institute for Security Cooperation. In 1988, Timothy McVeigh, Terry Nichols and Michael Fortier (the Oklahoma City bombing conspirators) met while in training at Fort Benning.

Since 1918, Fort Benning has served as the home of the infantry. Since 1940, Fort Knox, Kentucky, has served as the home of armor. Fort Benning's transformation to the Maneuver Center of Excellence is the result of the 2005 Base Realignment and Closure (BRAC) Commission's decision to move the armor school from Fort Knox to Fort Benning. The MCoE groundbreaking ceremony was held in February 2008.

Since September 11, 2001, Fort Benning has no longer been an open base because of the terrorist attacks that occurred, making public access into the post difficult. One of the major effects was the closure of various "attractions" normally visited by the public. Among one of the early victims was the National Infantry Museum. The National Infantry Museum, established at the home of the U.S. infantry in 1959, has just one mission: to honor the infantryman and his more than two centuries of proud service to the nation. It was housed in one of the barracks buildings built prior to the Second World War. The National Infantry Museum was closed after 9-11 and later relocated outside of the post's gates. The new museum is a state-of-the-art facility with an interesting outdoor exhibit of buildings relocated there from various parts of Fort Benning.

The World War II Company Street area is a seven-building complex. The wooden "series 700" buildings were mass produced in the 1940s to meet the demands of the burgeoning army. After World War II, installations continued to use the structures but they were rapidly being demolished. One of each kind of building was saved from Fort Benning and reassembled next to the National Infantry Museum and Soldier Center. The barracks, mess hall, orderly room, supply room, chapel, General George Patton's headquarters building and sleeping quarters are the only fully preserved set of series 700 buildings in existence. The structures are fully furnished with realistic touches like period music, photos and furniture. A Sherman tank and period physical training (PT) field add to the realism. It's a place that really comes to life for kids and serves as a window into that time in American history.

FORT STEWART

In June 1940, Congress authorized funding for the purchase of property in coastal Georgia for the purpose of building an antiaircraft artillery training center. It was to be located just outside of Hinesville, Georgia, some forty miles southwest of Savannah. The coming of the antiaircraft training center

A view of the headquarters for Fort Stewart. *AdeQ Historical Archives.*

to the area adjacent to the sleepy little community of Hinesville would forever alter its lifestyle. Hinesville, the county seat of Liberty County, was populated by barely five hundred people. It wasn't a particularly prosperous area; however, that had not always been the case.

Liberty County was rich in history, having provided two of Georgia's three signers of the Declaration of Independence. The area had always stood proudly for the cause of liberty, hence its name. Before the Civil War, it had been a very rich and prosperous area. That war had not affected the area much until the U.S. Army arrived with General William Tecumseh Sherman. In a matter of a few months, Liberty County was devastated. Its economy never recovered from that terrible blow. However, seventy-five years later, the U.S. Army returned, almost as if to make amends for that which it had been responsible for during the Civil War. The new post would mean new jobs, new industry and a major boost to the local economy, which was still suffering from the Great Depression. Hinesville would never be the same, and its fortunes would become entwined with those of the new post.

On July 1, 1940, the first 5,000 acres were bought, and subsequent purchases followed. Eventually the reservation would include over 280,000 acres and stretch over five counties. The large expanse of property was required for the firing ranges and impact areas that an antiaircraft artillery training center would need for live fire training. In November 1940, the center was officially designated as Camp Stewart in honor of General Daniel Stewart, a native of Liberty County who had fought with Francis Marion during the Revolution and became one of the county's military heroes. An announcement of the new post's name was made in January 1941.

During the early months, training was done on wooden mock-ups since real antiaircraft guns were in short supply. Live firing exercises were conducted on the beaches of St. Augustine and Amelia Island, Florida, since the necessary ranges and impact areas had not been completed at Camp Stewart. This live fire training over the ocean continued until September 1941, while at Camp Stewart practice firing and searchlight training progressed.

In the fall of 1941, the Carolina maneuvers were held, and all the antiaircraft units from Camp Stewart anticipated. As these maneuvers drew to a close, a feeling of restless anticipation pervaded the ranks of the National Guard soldiers who were looking toward their impending release from active duty after completion of their year of training. But the Japanese attack on Pearl Harbor on December 7 ended these dreams. Now the United States was in the war, and Camp Stewart set about accomplishing the mission it was intended for.

The National Guard units departed, and new units came in for training. Facilities were expanded and improved. Antiaircraft artillery training was upgraded, and soon a detachment of Women's Air Service Pilots (WASPs) arrived at the air facility on post, Liberty Field, to fly planes to tow targets for the live fire exercises. Eventually, radio-controlled airplane targets came into use as a more effective and safer means of live fire practice.

As the war progressed, Camp Stewart's training programs continued expanding to keep pace with the needs placed upon it. Units were shipped out promptly upon completion of their training, and new units received in their place. The camp provided well-trained soldiers for duty in Europe, the Mediterranean, North Africa and the Pacific theaters.

By late 1943, Camp Stewart had assumed a new responsibility as one of many holding areas designated in this country for German and Italian prisoners of war who had fallen into Allied hands during fighting in North Africa. These men were held in two separate prisoner of war facilities on post and used as a labor force for base operations, construction projects and for area farmers.

Beside its initial purposes as an antiaircraft artillery training center, Camp Stewart also served as a cook and bakers school and as a staging area for a number of army postal units. By spring 1944, the camp was bulging at its seams as more than fifty-five thousand soldiers occupied the facility during the buildup for the D-Day invasion. However, almost overnight, the post was virtually emptied as these units shipped out for England. With the D-Day invasion and Allied control of the air over Europe, the need for antiaircraft units diminished, and in response, the antiaircraft training at Camp Stewart was phased out. By January 1945, only the prisoner of war camp was still functioning.

With the end of the war, Camp Stewart came to life briefly as a separation center for redeployed soldiers, but on September 30, 1945, the post was inactivated. Only two officers, ten enlisted men and fifty civilian employees maintained the facilities, and the Georgia National Guard did the only training during summer months. It seemed as if Camp Stewart had served its purpose.

However, once again, world affairs affected the life of Camp Stewart. With the outbreak of hostilities in Korea in June 1950, the United States once again found itself with the need to update training and prepare new soldiers to meet the crisis in Korea. Camp Stewart was reopened on August 9, 1950, its facilities repaired and National Guard troops brought in for training. On December 28, 1950, Camp Stewart was redesignated as the Third Army Antiaircraft Artillery Training Center. Intensive training of soldiers destined for service in Korea began. Since control of the air in Korea wasn't seriously challenged by the Communist forces, in late 1953, Camp Stewart's role changed from solely antiaircraft training to include armor and tank firing as well.

When the Korean conflict eventually cooled down, it was recognized that our country would be required to maintain a ready and able military force to deal with any potential threat to the free world. Camp Stewart would have a role to play in that mission. The decision was made that the post would no longer be viewed as a temporary installation. On March 21, 1956, it was redesignated as Fort Stewart. Its role would continue to evolve in response to specific needs and world events.

In 1959, Fort Stewart was redesignated as an armor and artillery firing center, since its old antiaircraft ranges and impact areas were better suited for this purpose than for the new age of missiles. By 1961, there was a feeling that Fort Stewart may have served its usefulness, and there was movement afoot to deactivate the post again. However, the age of missiles brought with it new threats and a new place for Fort Stewart.

In late 1962, the United States was shocked to discover Russian offensive missiles being placed in Cuba. This revelation eventually led the world to the brink of war as the two superpowers stood toe to toe, each refusing to back away. The United States demanded the removal of these missiles, and Russia refused to comply. In response to this threat, the U.S. military began a rapid mobilization for possible use against Cuba. The First Armored Division was ordered to Fort Stewart for staging, and in the short span of two weeks, the population of the post rose from 3,500 personnel to over 30,000.

The country prepared for the worst, but in the end a compromise was reached, and the crisis passed. Shortly after, word was received at Fort Stewart that a VIP would be visiting the post and that the post conference room wasn't worthy of a person of this stature. Thus, preparations were rapidly made to convert this conference room into a more suitable one. The command group at Fort Stewart quickly discerned that this VIP would be none other than our nation's president, John F. Kennedy. He arrived at Hunter Field on November 26, 1962, and flew to Donovan Parade Field at Fort Stewart, where he reviewed the entire First Armored Division. From there he was taken to the new conference room, where he was briefed on armed forces readiness to respond to the Cuban missile crisis, and then he visited troops in nearby training areas.

After the Cuban missile crisis had passed, the cold war situation kept Fort Stewart in an active training role. During the late 1960s, another developing situation would bring about yet another change in Fort Stewart's mission. With tensions growing in the divided country of Vietnam, the United States found itself becoming increasingly involved in that conflict.

The Vietnamese terrain and the type of war being fought there demanded an increased aviation capability through the use of helicopters and light, fixed wing aircraft. This brought about a need for more aviators. In response to this need, an element of the U.S. Army Aviation School at Fort Rucker, Alabama, was transferred to Fort Stewart in 1966. Helicopter pilot training and helicopter gunnery courses became Fort Stewart's new mission. In an ironic twist, now instead of training soldiers to shoot down aircraft, they were training soldiers to fly them.

When the U.S. Air Force closed its base at Hunter Field in Savannah in 1967, the army promptly assumed control, and in conjunction with the flight training being conducted at Fort Stewart, the U.S. Army Flight Training Center came into being. The helicopter pilot training was rapidly accelerated, and pilots were trained and soon sent to duty all over the world, with a large percentage seeing active duty in Vietnam.

In 1969, President Nixon planned to reduce American involvement in Vietnam by training the Vietnamese military to take over the war. In conjunction with this, helicopter flight training for Vietnamese pilots began at the training center in 1970 and continued until 1972.

Gradually, America's involvement in Vietnam dwindled, and by mid-1972, the flight training aspect of Fort Stewart's mission was terminated and both Hunter Field and Fort Stewart reverted to garrison status. The following year, Hunter was closed entirely, and Fort Stewart sat idle with the exception of the National Guard training, which continued to be conducted at the installation.

It appeared as if Fort Stewart had once again reached the end of its usefulness and questions were raised about its status and future. The end of the Vietnam conflict meant a new focus for the U.S. Army, and a new life for several of the army's historic units would mean new life for Fort Stewart.

On July 1, 1974, the First Battalion, Seventy-fifth Infantry Regiment (Ranger), parachuted into Fort Stewart and was reactivated the following month. It was the first army ranger unit activated since World War II. Hunter Army Airfield was once again reopened to support the training and activities of the Rangers.

In October 1974, the headquarters, First Brigade of the Twenty-fourth Infantry Division, was activated at Fort Stewart. This historic unit, which had seen active and arduous service in the Pacific during World War II and in the Korean War, had been inactive since 1970. The "Victory" Division, as it was known, was going to make Fort Stewart its home, and it was perhaps fitting given the V-shaped layout of the main post itself. The Twenty-fourth Infantry Division would make Fort Stewart uniquely its own.

With the reactivation of the Twenty-fourth Infantry Division, the post entered a new phase in its history. Facilities were upgraded, and new permanent structures replaced many of the old wooden buildings from the days of Camp Stewart. On October 1, 1980, the Twenty-fourth Infantry Division was designated a mechanized division and assigned as the heavy infantry division of the newly organized Rapid Deployment Force. This designation was the fruition of that potential first realized by those who served at the post during the Cuban missile crisis.

The Twenty-fourth Infantry Division began intensive training over the expanse of piney woods and lowlands of the post and conducted live fire exercises on many of the old Camp Stewart antiaircraft ranges. Additional deployment training and exercises took division units from Georgia's woodlands to the National Guard Training Center in California, as well as to other areas of the world such as Egypt and Turkey. Their training was continuous. The mission of the Rapid Deployment Force was to be prepared to deploy to practically any point on the globe at a moment's notice to deal with whatever threat might be discerned.

In August 1990, Iraq invaded and overran neighboring Kuwait and threatened to do the same to Saudi Arabia. The Port of Savannah worked around the clock to load and ship the division's heavy equipment, while aircraft shuttles from Hunter Field flew the division's personnel to Saudi Arabia. Within a month, the entire division had been reassembled in Saudi Arabia to face the possible invasion of that country by Iraqi forces. Fort Stewart saw a growing influx of National Guard and Reserve units who were being mobilized to support the operations in Saudi Arabia and to assume the tasks at the post that had formerly been accomplished by division personnel. In many ways, Fort Stewart appeared to be almost a ghost town, as never before had the entire division been deployed from the post at one time. Within eight months, the crisis in the Persian Gulf had concluded, and the Twenty-fourth Infantry Division triumphantly returned to its home in coastal Georgia.

On April 25, 1996, the Third Infantry Division was activated at Fort Stewart. This began a new chapter in the history of Fort Stewart. After many years of up and down cycles of activity and inactivity, Fort Stewart has become a permanent post, providing important training to its soldiers and assistance to its neighbors in coastal Georgia. In its years of service, it has provided support for four of America's conflicts and looks confidently to the future to continue servicing its nation, its people and its soldiers. Fort Stewart also is a leading mobilization station for army units preparing for tours in Operation Iraqi Freedom as well as two-week National Guard annual training.

Today, Fort Stewart is the largest army installation east of the Mississippi River. It covers 279,270 acres, which include parts of Liberty, Long, Bryan, Evans and Tattnall Counties. The reservation is about thirty-nine miles across from east to west and nineteen miles from north to south. Stewart has it all: size, terrain, climate and location. It's close to the East Coast and two deep-water ports: Savannah and Charleston, South Carolina. Tank, field artillery, helicopter gunnery and small arms ranges operate simultaneously throughout the year with little time lost to bad weather. Hunter Army Airfield, part of the Stewart/Hunter complex, is located in Savannah, covers about 5,400 acres and is also the home of the U.S. Coast Guard Station, Savannah—the largest helicopter unit in the Coast Guard. It provides Savannah and the Southeast United States with round-the-clock search and rescue coverage of its coastal areas.

HUNTER ARMY AIR FIELD

In 1929, the general aviation committee of the Savannah City Council recommended that the 730-acre Belmont Tract, belonging to J.C. Lewis, be accepted by the council as the future site of the Savannah Municipal Airport. The coast of the land was $35,000. By September 1929, the runway and several buildings were ready, and the city officially opened the new facility.

The airport became part of Eastern Air Transport Incorporated intrastate route on December 2, 1931, when Miss Ida Hoynes, daughter of the Mayor and Mrs. Thomas M. Hoynes, broke a bottle of Savannah River water on a propeller blade of an eighteen-passenger Curtiss Condor during the christening ceremony.

The airport was named Hunter Municipal Airfield in May 1940 during Savannah Aviation Week in honor of Lieutenant Colonel Frank O'Driscoll Hunter, a Savannahian and World War I flying ace. Lieutenant Colonel Hunter, who would later climb to the rank of major general, was not scheduled to appear in Savannah that week. However, he paid a surprise visit to the field on the first day of Aviation Week while en route to France to serve as a United States military air attaché.

Washington gave the U.S. Army Air Corps approval to build a base at Hunter on August 30, 1940. The Third and Twenty-seventh Bombardment Groups and the Thirty-fifth Air Base Group with 2,700 soldiers from Barksdale Field, Louisiana, were the first tenants. Official dedication of the base, renamed Savannah Air Base, took place February 19, 1941.

The base was an operational training unit for several years. B-10s, B-18s and B-23s gave way to A-20s, P-38s and P-40s as the air arm of the nation matured. It later became a final staging base for B-17 crews on their way to the European theater of operations. The army's Eighth Air Force was activated at Savannah Air Base during that period.

At the end of the war, the field was used as a separation center until its return to the City of Savannah in June 1946. Hunter returned to its peacetime role as a civilian airport. Many of its buildings were leased to industrial plants. Some of them became apartment houses. An orphanage was located in the commanding officer's quarters, and the University of Georgia established an extension campus on part of the old base.

In 1949, the recently reactivated Second Bomb Wing was moved from Tucson, Arizona, to Savannah's Chatham Air Force Base. The limited facilities at the base, located eight miles northwest of Savannah, made the site unfit for permanent use. Rather than see the air force move elsewhere, Savannah offered to exchange airfields with the federal government. The city and county governments purchased 3,500 acres of additional land around Hunter for future base expansions. Following a token payment of one dollar to make the transaction legal, Hunter was back in uniform in September 1950 as an air force installation.

The Department of Defense announced in 1964 that the base, along with ninety-four other military installations, would be closed. The base was given a period of three years to phase out.

In December 1966, at the height of the Vietnam conflict, the Department of the Army announced that the secretary of defense had approved an increase in the number of army helicopter pilots to be trained. Because of this increase, coupled with the fact that the United States Army Aviation School at Fort Rucker, Alabama, was operating at capacity, Hunter Air Force Base was turned over to the army and operated in conjunction with Fort Stewart, located forty miles southwest of Hunter. Brigadier General Frank Meszar, commanding general of Fort Stewart, formally accepted the base from Colonel James A. Evans Jr., commanding officer at Hunter, in a formal change of command and service ceremony on April 1, 1967.

The headquarters of the U.S. Army Aviation School Element, which was established at Fort Stewart during the summer of 1966 to train fixed-wing pilots, was moved to Hunter. The mission of the element was to coordinate the training of fixed-wing and rotary-wing aviators as an extension of the army's training program at Fort Rucker and Fort Wolters, Texas.

On July 28, 1967, the combined facilities of Fort Stewart and Hunter Army Airfield were redesignated the United States Army Flight Training Center.

Advanced helicopter training for Republic of Vietnam air force students began March 13, 1970, with the arrival of the first class of students. Concurrent with the increase in the Vietnamese student input, flight training for U.S. Army officers and warrant officers was gradually phased out. The final class was on June 16, 1970.

In 1973, Hunter Army Airfield went into caretaker status. It was reopened in 1975 as a support facility for the reactivated Twenty-fourth Infantry Division (Mechanized), at Fort Stewart. The Twenty-fourth Infantry Division (Mechanized), or Victory Division, became part of the nation's Rapid Deployment Force on October 1, 1980.

The Victory Division's ability to deploy on short notice was enhanced by Hunter's 11,340-foot runway (the army's longest runway east of the Mississippi River and capable of accommodating the air force's C-5 Galaxy transport aircraft), Savannah's deep-water port facility and excellent rail and road networks.

The Twenty-fourth Infantry Division's rapid deployment capability was put to the supreme test in 1990 after Iraq invaded Kuwait. Alerted on August 7, the first soldiers of the division deployed from Hunter Army Airfield in just six days. Six and a half months later, on February 24, 1991, the division attacked 370 kilometers deep into the enemy's flank and rear. Moving farther and faster than any other mechanized force in military history, the Twenty-fourth severed Iraqi lines of communication with Baghdad and systematically destroyed six Iraqi divisions while taking more than five thousand prisoners.

Currently, Hunter Army Airfield has approximately five thousand soldiers on station. It is home for units of the Third Infantry Division (Mechanized) headquartered at Fort Stewart. There are also a number of non-divisional units assigned to Hunter. The major divisional units stationed at Hunter include the 3rd Aviation Brigade and 603rd Aviation Support Battalion. Non-divisional units that make up the major tenant units include the 260th Quartermaster Battalion; the 1st Battalion, 75th Ranger Regiment; 3rd Battalion, 160th Special Operations Aviation Regiment (Airborne); and the 224th Military Intelligence Battalion (Aerial Exploitation).

The Coast Guard Air Station Savannah is also located on Hunter Army Airfield. It is the largest helicopter unit in the Coast Guard and provides Savannah and coastal Georgia with round-the-clock search and rescue coverage of the area.

Naval Air Station Atlanta

Anticipating America's involvement in a second world war, the government returned to the site of Camp Gordon in October 1940 and over the next seven months constructed a four-hundred-acre Naval Reserve Aviation Base at the DeKalb County Airport.

Commissioned in March 1941, the field's chief mission was primary flight training of navy and marine corps aviators. Expanding to meet war needs, the base added training for instrument flight instructors and in January 1943 was designated Naval Air Station (NAS) Atlanta. Training some three thousand pilots and over four thousand instructors, NAS Atlanta supported the vast expansion of naval aviation that proved decisive in the Pacific war against Japan.

Following World War II, NAS Atlanta became a Reserve Naval Air Station with nine squadrons (F4U Corsairs, F6F Hellcats, TMB Avengers and PBY Catalinas) and trained reservists to meet the Korean War emergency of 1950–53.

The evolution of jet fighters and large patrol bombers prompted the relocation of NAS Atlanta to the longer runways of Dobbins Air Force Base, Marietta, in 1959. The Naval Air State Historical Marker is located inside the main entrance to DeKalb-Peachtree Airport near the intersection of Airport and Clairmont Roads (DeKalb County).

Albany Army Air Field

Albany Airport opened in 1935 about four miles southwest of the city. In October 1938, Eastern Air Lines began mail service to the field. Eastern's Eddie Rickenbacker announced that as soon as the city improved the airport, his airline would start passenger service. The city was doing just that during 1939 and 1940 in the form of a WPA project to enlarge the landing area and build a passenger terminal.

In 1940, the United States Army Air Corps was establishing civilian pilot training schools at airports in the Southeast, which was an ideal location because of its moderate weather. Previously, Albany Airport had been rejected as an advanced training base (Turner Army Airfield was built north of Albany instead), but the army approved Albany Airport for a primary contract school in June. The city agreed to provide $500,000 for further improvements to the landing field, the completion of the passenger terminal, the cost of constructing two hangars and half the cost of a third hangar. An additional investment of over $400,000 was made by Hal S. Darr, owner of the contract flying school, for the construction of the cantonment area and half the cost of one hangar. Ground was broken in July 1940. The army air corps named the school the Fifty-second Army Air Force Fight Training Detachment. Thus, Darr Aero Tech became the first army air corps activity constructed in Georgia during the buildup to World War II.

On August 15, 1940, the first class of forty-five cadets began training. The cadets were initially housed in the Georgia Hotel until the barracks reached completion on August 20. Flight training commenced with fifteen PT-13 Stearmans and eleven flight instructors. Seven classes of American cadets were trained until July 1941. On June 8, 1941, the school received the first British RAF cadets. For the next fourteen months, Darr's classes were exclusively British. A conflict existed between Turner and Darr over airspace. Generally, Turner's airspace was located north of Albany and Darr's south of Albany. Where the areas overlapped, Turner's aircraft flew above five thousand feet and Darr's below five thousand. Darr's three auxiliary fields were located south of Albany.

During the first year of operation, Darr Aero Tech graduated 559 American and 86 British cadets. The last British class graduated on October 10, 1942. The 7 British cadets killed at Darr and Turner Field were interred at Albany's Crown Hill Cemetery. A granite monument and flagpole mark the graves today.

On December 11, 1941, the Defense Plant Corporation bought the school from Mr. Darr for $408,000, and the airfield was called Albany Army Airfield. Anticipating an increase in training, an additional $100,000 was spent on improvements in 1942 that included a dispensary, cold storage building, additional barracks and a Link Trainer building. After the end of 1943, training began to decrease, eventually ending with the closing of the school on December 28, 1944.

In September 1945, control of the airfield was turned over to the City of Albany, and Eastern resumed service after the war. The airport eventually received paved runways. In 2004, the only structures of Darr Aero Tech remaining are the three hangars. No trace of the cantonment area exists. In 1959, a new terminal building was completed and named in honor of the then mayor William McAfee. Albany Army Airfield and Darr Aero Tech were remembered by a display inside the terminal building, as well as a memorial and flagpole outside.

Camp Toccoa

The camp, located five miles from Toccoa, was first planned in 1938 and constructed by the Georgia National Guard and the Works Projects Administration beginning January 17, 1940. The Georgia National Guard camp was dedicated on December 14, 1940. The facility was initially named Camp General Robert Toombs after a Confederate Civil War general. In 1942, the U.S. Army took over the site. There were very few buildings or facilities there, and original personnel were housed in tents. More permanent barracks were built as the first soldiers started to arrive. The story goes that Colonel Robert Sink, commander of one of the first units to train there, the 506th Parachute Infantry Regiment (PIR), thought that it was bad psychology to have young men arrive at Toccoa by traveling Route 13 past a casket factory (the Toccoa Casket Company) to learn to jump at Camp "Tombs," so he persuaded the Department of the Army to change the name to Camp Toccoa.

World War II memorial mounted on the pedestal mounts that once held a whippet tank and marked the entrance into Camp Toccoa.

The only standing structure of Camp Toccoa.

Initially, Camp Toccoa used the Toccoa municipal airport for jump training, but due to a transport accident, it was abandoned for having too short a runway for safe C-39 and C-47 operations. All further jump training occurred at Fort Benning, Georgia. Camp Toccoa also lacked a rifle range, so airborne trainees would march thirty miles to Clemson Agricultural College, a military school in South Carolina, to practice on the college's shooting range.

The most prominent local landmark is Currahee Mountain. Paratroopers in training ran from the camp up the mountain and back, as memorialized in the HBO series *Band of Brothers*, with the shout "three miles up, three miles down." Members of the 506th refer to themselves as "Currahees," derived from the Cherokee word *gurahiyi*, which may mean "standing alone." The crest is surmounted by a group of telecommunications towers.

The following units were trained at Camp Toccoa: 501st PIR (attached to the U.S. 101st Airborne Division); 506th PIR (attached to the U.S. 101st Airborne Division); 507th PIR (attached to the U.S. 82nd Airborne Division and the U.S. 17th Airborne Division); 511th PIR (attached to the U.S. 11th

Airborne Division); 517th PIR (attached to the U.S. 17th Airborne Division and the U.S. 13th Airborne Division); 457th Parachute Field Artillery Battalion (attached to the U.S. 11th Airborne Division); and 295th Ordnance Heavy Maintenance Company (FA) (completed basic training at Camp Toccoa from July 21, 1943, through November 24, 1943).

The camp closed at the end of the war. In the late 1940s, it served as a Georgia State Prison site, housing primarily youthful offenders, but several escapes forced the state to close the site, moving the operation to a new facility at Alto, Georgia. The twisting trail up Currahee is now named for Colonel Sink. The only remaining building from the camp is the mess hall, which sits on a corner of a Milliken & Company textile plant. The Patterson Pump Company occupies another portion of the grounds. The concrete foundation upon which formed the base for a World War I whippet tank was once the camp's entrance and is now marked with a memorial to the paratroopers who trained there.

Today, the history and artifacts from Camp Toccoa and the men who trained there are preserved at the Currahee Military Museum, appropriately located in the town's newly renovated train depot, where all World War II paratroopers arrived before hiking to the camp to begin training. On displays at the museum are medals, photos, maps, weapons and military uniforms, but it is the old stable that most visitors come to see. Built in Aldbourne, England, in 1922, it is one of the actual stables that housed both Able and Easy Companies of the 506th before and after D-Day. Many veterans who lived in the stables returned to England to visit the site after the war. One by one the stables were torn down until only one remained. Realizing the historical significance of the structure, the owner offered it to the Town of Toccoa, which arranged for it to be disassembled, flown to the United States and reassembled inside the museum.

Cochran Army Air Field

Early in 1940, the Macon Chamber of Commerce began a campaign to bring war industries and defense installations to the city. Negotiations with the army air corps resulted in a tract of land in a highly developed agricultural area nine miles south of the city known as Avondale being selected by the air corps.

The City of Macon and Bibb County obtained options on the desired tracts of land. Once the army air corps finally decided to build an airbase

Interior view of a typical enlisted men's barracks during World War II. This photo is identified as being taken in Byron Field (Cochran AAF Aux No. 4) near Byron in 1944. This was an auxiliary field for Cochran Army Airfield near Macon. *AdeQ Historical Archives*.

Entrance to Cochran Field during World War II. It opened in 1941 and served until 1947. Today it is the site of the Middle Georgia Regional Airport near Macon. *AdeQ Historical Archives*.

at the site, it required the base be built as soon as possible. An informal agreement with the army stipulated that when the War Department had no further use for the property, the deed would revert to the city and the county. On February 19, 1941, the army awarded a general contract for the construction of necessary temporary buildings, barracks, grading and paving of the runways and parking apron. Ground was broken on March 4, 1941. Construction proceeded at a rapid rate, only slowed at times by the delay in delivery of construction materials. The cantonment area, typical in size to other basic training schools of the war, had accommodations for 190 officers, 475 cadets and 1,660 enlisted men. The original plan called for administration buildings, thirteen cadet barracks, thirty-five enlisted barracks, four bachelor officers' quarters (BOQs), six mess halls and various other structures to support a complement of 216 airplanes.

The airfield was named Cochran Army Airfield in memory of Camilla, Georgia native Lieutenant Robert J. Cochran of the Eighth Aero Squadron, who lost his life in World War I. It was assigned to the AAF Southeast Training Center. Unlike other army airfields, Cochran only had two paved runways, each 300 feet wide by 4,500 feet long, provided on the seven-hundred-acre landing area. No hangars were provided by the original plan. The parking apron or ramp was 450 feet by 2,500 feet.

An original cadre consisting of an advanced detachment of three officers and sixty-five enlisted men arrived from Gunter Field, Alabama, on April 15, 1941. These squadrons had been originally formed at Maxwell Field before being sent to Gunter for training in the various squadron functions. Although far from complete, the Army Air Force Pilot School (Basic) at Macon, Georgia, activated on May 15, 1941. The first three Vultee BT-13 Valiants arrived at Cochran on May 23 for instructor training and familiarization. The official opening of the field occurred on May 31 when a formation of fifty BT-13s flew over downtown Macon before landing at Cochran. The press and the people of Macon celebrated the occasion. Of the fifty aircraft, half remained on loan, while the remainder was returned to Gunter.

Cochran AAF had several auxiliary support airfields under its control: Cochran AAF Aux No. 1—(Gunn Field), Cochran AAF Aux No. 2—(Perry Field), Cochran AAF Aux No. 3—(Harris Field), Cochran AAF Aux No. 4—(Byron Field) and Cochran AAF Aux No. 5—(Myrtle Field).

On June 3, 1941, ninety-seven cadets from Class 41-H arrived after completing primary training at Souther Army Airfield in Americus, Turner Army Airfield in Albany and Arcadia Army Airfield in Florida. The AAF named cadet classes for the projected time of finishing training during a particular year. Since the barracks had not been completed, tents provided initial housing. Flight training began on June 4, three days ahead of schedule, from an unpaved area at the southeast corner of the field, away from the runway construction. Tents also provided the cadet squadron quarters and an operations office. This situation slowly improved with the paving of the base's streets. The operations building and cadet squadron building reached completion at the end of June, followed by the opening of the runways in early July.

On August 17, 1941, the first class of British Royal Air Force cadets arrived at Cochran Field. Until June 1942, Cochran was used exclusively for British training. Liaison was maintained between the RAF and the U.S. Army Air Force through a Royal Air Force administrative officer. British cadets differed significantly from American cadets. Firstly, British physical requirements were much lower than for American cadets. The British were either from seventeen to twenty-one years of age or over twenty-seven years old. Many of the older cadets, married with children, worried about their families back home. The giving of tactical training and attendant discipline, along American lines and pursuant to traditional American policy, concerned and irritated the British cadets. They believed that if they had to be trained in the United States, they should be subject to British discipline and be taught British tactics—the Americans should handle flight training only. In addition, unlike American cadets who grew up operating a farm tractor or automobile, the most complicated device operated by the average British cadet was a bicycle. Some training bases reportedly taught British cadets how to operate a motorcycle before attempting any flight training. The last British cadets completed training in the United States in March 1943. With the last British class graduating in early 1943, the War Department constituted and activated the Twenty-seventh Flying Training Wing (Basic) at Cochran and assigned it to the (redesignated) AAF Eastern Flying Training Command as a flying training unit. Peak training took place during 1943. From the beginning of 1944, flight training steadily diminished.

Cochran ended basic training on March 15, 1945. The AAF used the cantonment area as a convalescent hospital and as a separation center after the war ended. The air force inactivated the base on December 15, 1945. Cochran Field, however, was used as a communications base until finally being closed on January 1, 1947. Following the war, Cochran was utilized for various purposes. Smart Field remained as Macon's municipal airport until 1947. After a tornado swept Smart Field, the airlines moved their operations to Cochran, where they remain to this day. The passenger terminal was built in 1959 and extensively renovated in 2003. Commercial airline service to this airport included Eastern Airlines and Delta Air Lines with its ASA "Delta Connection" discontinuing service to the airport in 2008. The former names of this airport were Lewis B. Wilson Municipal Airport and Macon Municipal Airport. It is currently (2011) known as Middle Georgia Regional Airport. The two army-built hangars still exist, along with a few old warehouses. The air force still has a presence at the airport with a Georgia Air Guard non-flying engineering unit.

FORT GILLEM

Fort Gillem is a United States Army military base located in Forest Park, Georgia, on the southeast edge of Atlanta. Founded in 1941, it is a satellite installation of nearby Fort McPherson. The base houses many different supply and support units, including the U.S. Army Criminal Investigation Laboratory and the Third MP Group (CID), both units of the United States Army Criminal Investigation Command. It employs 456 active duty personnel, 1,663 army reservists and 1,667 civilians.

In 1973, its 1,465 acres (5.93 kilometers square) were annexed by Forest Park. The fort was named in the memory of Lieutenant General Alvan Cullom Gillem Jr. On May 13, 2005, the Base Realignment and Closure Commission recommended that this base be closed. This may be subject to change by the president of the United States and the United States Congress. Fort Gillem is currently (2011) home to First U.S. Army, the Army and Air Force Exchange Service (Atlanta Distribution Center), Third Military Police Group (CID) United States Army Criminal Investigation Command, Second Recruiting Brigade, Fifty-second Ordnance Group and the Equipment Concentration Site for the Eighty-first Regional Support Command. Many army, Department of Defense and government organizations call Fort Gillem home.

MOODY AIR FORCE BASE

The base had its beginning in 1940 when a group of concerned Valdosta and Lowndes County citizens began searching for a way to assist the expanding defense program. The citizens rallied interest in the War Department for

Scenes of Moody Air Force Base during the cold war years. *AdeQ Historical Archives.*

a 9,300-acre tract formerly known as the Lakeland Flatwoods Project, northeast of Valdosta. On May 14, 1941, the War Department was granted exclusive use of the land by the Agriculture Department.

The base's primary mission in its early years was to meet the requirements of the Air Force Pilot Instrument School and Instrument Flying School. On February 19, 1942, the Moody Field Advanced Pilot Training School began training fifty army air corps cadets in the Beech AT-10. Following World War II in November 1947, Moody was placed on inactive status but was reactivated in May 1951 when the Korean conflict created a need for more air force pilots.

In September 1975, the 347th Tactical Fighter Wing, belonging to the Tactical Air Command, relocated from Thailand to Moody. In December 1975, the 347th TFW formally replaced the 38th Flying Training Wing at Moody, flying the F-4E Phantom II as the primary mission.

On October 1, 1991, the 347th TFW was redesignated as the 347th Fighter Wing. The 347th Fighter Wing was assigned to the Air Combat Command in June 1992. On July 1, 1994, the air force converted the 347th Fighter Wing to the 347th Wing, a force projection, airland composite wing.

On May 8, 2001, the 347th Wing was converted to the 347th Rescue Wing, becoming the air force's only active-duty combat search and rescue wing. On October 1, 2003, the 347th RQW was realigned from Air Combat

Command to Air Force Special Operations Command in an effort to bring all Combat Search and Rescue (CSAR) assets under one major command.

On April 3, 2006, the 347th RQW was realigned from AFSOC to Air Combat Command to link CSAR assets directly to the combat air forces and the personnel they support. On October 1, 2006, the Air Force redesignated the 347th RQW as the 347th Rescue Group and assigned it to the Twenty-third Wing, which officially became the host unit at Moody on the same day. Along with the Twenty-third Wing designation, the base accepted the responsibility of carrying on the historic Flying Tiger's heritage.

Among many other achievements, host wings stationed at Moody won the commander in chief's Installation Excellence Award for 1991 and the 1994 Verne Orr Award, which is presented by the Air Force Association to the unit that most effectively uses human resources to accomplish its mission. In September 2008, Air Combat Command awarded the Twenty-third Wing with the Air Force Outstanding Unit Award for the ninth time in its illustrious history.

The tenant units of Moody Air Force Base are as follows: 93rd Air Ground Operations Wing; Area Defense Counsel; 336th Recruiting Squadron; 372nd Training Squadron, Detachment 9; Air Force Office of Special Investigations Detachment 311.

Bainbridge Army Air Field

The army constructed a basic flight training field on a 2,053-acre tract in August 1942. It remained open until 1945. At its peak, 9,600 officers, enlisted men, trainees and WACs were stationed at this base. There were 700 civilian employees, and several hundred German POWs were imprisoned there. In

Bainbridge Air Base opened in 1942 and served as a military airfield until 1961. It is now the site of the Decatur County Industrial Air Park. *AdeQ Historical Archives.*

1951, Southern Airways School, a private company, contracted with the air force to train its pilots. The base closed in 1961 and became an industrial park. The Bainbridge Army Airfield Historical Marker is located on U.S. 27 at Bainbridge Industrial Park, four miles north of Bainbridge, Georgia (Decatur County).

CHATHAM ARMY AIRFIELD

Savannah/Hilton Head International Airport was originally named Chatham Field and developed as a Works Progress Administration project at Cherokee Hill, one of the highest elevations in Chatham County, Georgia. In 1939, Congress had instituted a program to improve the nation's airport infrastructure in the interest of national defense. If local governments provided the land, the federal government would fund construction of the airport. The city then approached the Civil Aeronautics Administration (CAA) about the possibility of building an airport at Cherokee Hill. The CAA accepted this proposal, informing the city that as much as $400,000 would be allocated for construction of three four-thousand-foot runways. The city purchased six hundred acres at the CAA-approved site seven miles northwest of town center for $20,000.

Base hospital area of Savannah Air Base during World War II. *AdeQ Historical Archives*.

Some of the few remaining World War II–era buildings left that now comprise the Savannah/Hilton Head International Airport.

By the time the project got underway in 1941, the United States was on an unalterable road to war, and the army air corps as well as the navy took an interest in the strategically located coastal airport. The United States Navy, looking for a blimp base in the area, attempted to gain control of the airfield. The air corps, on the other hand, wanted the airfield for an auxiliary of Hunter Field, located eight miles south. The Interdepartmental Air Traffic Control Board, consisting of members of the army, navy and CAA to resolve conflicts such as this between the services, sided with the air corps. The navy eventually built a blimp base at Brunswick, Georgia, seventy-five miles to the south.

With the air corps established already in the Savannah area at Hunter Field, work on Chatham proceeded at a slow pace. The construction project involved improving runways and airplane hangars, with three concrete runways, several taxiways and a large parking apron and a control tower being built. Several large hangars were also constructed. Buildings were ultimately utilitarian and quickly assembled. Most base buildings, not meant for long-term use, were constructed of temporary or semi-permanent materials. Although some hangars had steel frames and the occasional brick or tile brick building could be seen, most support buildings sat on concrete foundations but were of frame construction clad in little more than plywood and tarpaper. Chatham Army Airfield, named for its Georgia county location, was finally activated on September 19, 1943, over two years after construction began.

Initially a sub-base of Hunter Field, the air force intended Chatham AAF for use by Third Air Force, III Reconnaissance Command and the Army Air Forces Antisubmarine Command. In June 1943, the 100th Bombardment Squadron (Medium) was assigned to the airfield flying B-25 Mitchell bombers on antisubmarine patrols. However, in August, the antisubmarine patrol mission was transferred to the United States Navy.

Two days after the base's activation, First Air Force took over command and made Chatham a sub-base of Jacksonville AAF. First Air Force used Chatham for B-24 operational training. Although Chatham had an adequate airfield, the cantonment area was deemed lacking, with accommodations for only a reduced station complement and one tactical squadron. This presented a major problem, since insufficient facilities existed to accommodate a B-24 group scheduled to arrive in the latter part of October. Hard work by base personnel provided necessary facilities when the 460th Bombardment Group, consisting of the 760th, 761st, 762nd and 763rd Bombardment Squadrons, arrived on October 29, 1943.

After the 460th BG deployed to Fifteenth Air Force in Italy during January 1944. First Air Force changed Chatham's mission to replacement training. The 302nd Bombardment Group (355th, 356th, 357th and 420th) flying B-24s as the Operational Training Units, training replacement B-24 aircrews. The 460th was replaced by squadrons of the 302nd Bombardment Group (355th, 356th, 357th and 420th) flying B-24s as Operational Training Units, training replacement B-24 aircrews.

On May 1, 1945, Chatham AAF was transferred from the First to the Third Air Force. Among the eight generals present for the ceremony was Major General Frank Hunter, commander of the First Air Force, a Savannah native and the namesake of nearby Hunter Field. Among his acts that day, Hunter decorated eleven of Chatham's men.

Chatham's new mission under Third Air Force was a training base for the B-29 Superfortress. By July, twenty-nine B-29s were on hand. However, with the end of the war in 1945, Chatham AAF was no longer needed, and it was placed on inactive status on January 10, 1946, with the 324th Army Air Force Base Unit (Standby) assuming caretaker duties over the facility. The reconstituted Georgia Air National Guard stationed its 158th Fighter Squadron at Chatham Field on October 13, 1946, flying its P-47 Thunderbolts until 1949, when it moved to Hunter AFB to accommodate the active-duty air force.

On July 17, 1947, the United States Air Force reactivated the airfield. Chatham was assigned to Strategic Air Command, with the 380th Bombardment Group being assigned to jurisdiction of the base, and work was begun to modernize the airfield from its World War II wartime configuration into a permanent air force base with modern facilities. Although Chatham had an adequate airfield for B-29 operations, the cantonment area was in poor condition. Constructed to last for five years, the buildings had reached the end of their life expectancy. In addition, the buildings' shortcomings also included outside latrines and potbellied stoves for heating.

In January 1948, the base was renamed Chatham Air Force Base. On November 1, 1948, Boeing B-50 Superfortress aircraft were assigned to the base from the 307th Bombardment Group, with a mission being transition training of B-29 bomber crews to the new B-50. On March 1, 1949, Chatham was reassigned to Eighth Air Force, and the Second Bombardment Group was reassigned from Davis-Monthan AFB, Arizona, to Chatham, with B-50s.

The inadequacies of the support facilities at Chatham caused the air force to make the decision to either leave Chatham and move to Hunter or leave Savannah. The facilities at Hunter AFB were built in the 1930s to permanent specifications and made Hunter much more desirable than Chatham. The City of Savannah interceded with the air force and offered to trade the larger Hunter Field, then a municipal airport, for the smaller Chatham AFB to keep SAC and the USAF in Savannah. This arrangement was agreed to, and on September 29, 1950, the Second Bomb Group moved to Hunter AFB and Chatham was turned over to the City of Savannah.

Once back under civil control, the airport was renamed Travis Field, in honor of Savannah natives Brigadier General Robert F. Travis, killed in the crash of a B-29 near Fairfield-Suisun AFB, California, and his brother, Colonel William Travis. To accommodate the airlines, Travis Field received a new control tower and an airline terminal in the former base theater. In 1953, when the Air National Guard 158th Fighter Squadron returned from activation during the Korean War, it based at Travis Field. This required the extension of Travis's east–west runway to eight thousand feet for the Guard's F-84 Thunderjets. Today, the old airfield, renamed as the Savannah/Hilton Head International Airport, continues serving the military.

Savannah ANGB at Savannah/Hilton Head International Airport is home to the 165th Airlift Wing (165 AW), an Air Mobility Command (AMC)–gained unit of the Georgia Air National Guard, currently flying the C-130H Hercules tactical airlift aircraft. The wing consists of over nine hundred full-time active guard and reserve (AGR), air reserve technician (ART) and part-time "traditional" air national guardsmen, available for domestic operations as an air national guard unit or worldwide deployment in support of the U.S. Air Force and unified combatant commanders.

Savannah ANGB also hosts the Combat Readiness Training Center (CRTC). Located at Savannah/Hilton Head International Airport/Savannah ANGB, the CRTC is one of four such training facilities in the nation. The CRTC provides airspace and ranges, aircraft parking, aircraft ground equipment (AGE), maintenance areas, training facilities, dormitories and other support functions for regular U.S. Air Force, Air Force Reserve Command, Air National Guard, U.S. Navy, Navy Reserve, U.S. Marine Corps and Marine Corps Reserve tactical jet aviation units.

ROBINS AIR FORCE BASE

The War Department, in search of a site for an army air corps depot, selected the sleepy whistle-stop town of Welleston, Georgia, fifteen miles south of Macon. Army colonel Charles Thomas, originally from Atlanta, landed at the Herbert Smart Airport near Camp Wheeler (Macon) in October 1941 to oversee the building of the location that would later become the home to Welleston Air Depot at Robins Field (later to become Robins AFB).

It was Colonel Thomas who chose the name "Robins" for his mentor, Brigadier General Augustine Warner Robins. Brigadier General Robins is considered the "father of logistics" for his system of cataloging supplies and materials. He had a lengthy military career prior to becoming the chief of the Air Corps Materiel Division. Robins traveled in China disguised as a millionaire tourist, collecting intelligence for the army. He also went to Mexico, where he served under General John J. Pershing in the army's campaign against Pancho Villa. He trained during World War I to become a pilot, earning his wings in June 1918. He didn't get to see combat because the war was ending. Robins suffered a near-fatal plane crash in 1921 in which his jaw and arm were severely broken. He died of a heart attack on Father's Day, June 16, 1940, at Randolph Field, Texas, while he was commandant of the Air Corps Training Center.

A storm sewer drain cover bearing the early name of Welleston Air Depot. The military post would later be known as Robins Air Force Base. *Robins Air Force Base Museum of Aviation/ photo by the author.*

A C-130 Hercules cargo transport undergoing periodic maintenance at Robins Air Force Base near Macon during the cold war years. *AdeQ Historical Archives.*

This page: During the cold war, the army established Nike missile sites in Georgia. Detachments were in Robins AFB (A Battery: R-28 Nike Missile Base in Jeffersonville, and B Battery: R-88 Nike Missile Base in Byron) and in Turner AFB (TU-79 Nike Missile Base in Armenia/Sasse and TU-28 Nike Missile Base in Willingsham/Sylvester). Seen here are the facilities as they appear now since the end of the collapse of the Soviet Union in 1991: above is the R-88 Nike Missile Base in Byron, while below is the TU-28 Nike Missile Base near Sylvester. *AdeQ Historical Archives*.

Spurred on by the Japanese attack on Pearl Harbor in December 1941, the number of construction workers at Robins Field reached 2,200 by Christmas 1941. The army enlarged the project by purchasing 2,637 additional acres and leasing 782 more south of the depot for troop training. In May 1942, the number of construction workers peaked at 6,600. The contractors essentially completed the project by August 31, 1942. Construction on the industrial and cantonment areas was completed by August 31, 1942. The second and third phases were completed the following April.

The rapidly growing town of Wellston changed its name to Warner Robins on September 1, 1942. Known as the Georgia Air Depot in the beginning, the depot has undergone many name changes. It was redesignated seven times, eventually being named Warner Robins Army Air Depot on October 14, 1942.

Warner Robins Army Air Depot eventually assumed overall command of the Air Service Command's installations in the states of Georgia, South Carolina, a portion of Florida and North Carolina. Warner Robins supported approximately 6,500 army aircraft in this area with depot maintenance and supply.

Throughout World War II (1941–45), 23,670 employees repaired almost every kind of AAF aircraft, including B-17s, C-47s, B-29s, B-24s, P-38s, P-47s and P-51s. Its training facilities turned out nearly sixty thousand field repair mechanics for every theater of war. The workforce supplied every kind of part necessary to keep AAF planes flying, especially spark plugs. It also maintained thousands of parachutes, aircraft electronic and radio systems and AAF small arms.

In addition to aircraft maintenance and supply, air depots also trained aviation support personnel. These included air depot groups and air service groups, plus medical, military police, quartermaster, ordnance, chemical and signal personnel. Warner Robins sent its first trained unit, the Thirty-eighth Air Depot Group, overseas in December 1942. It is estimated that over fifty thousand army personnel trained at Warner Robins during the war.

The depot's complement began a steady decline after the war, and by March 1946, only 3,900 employees remained. In the postwar era, Robins assumed the task of storing surplus war material and thousands of vehicles. The depot also cocooned and stored 250 B-29s. On September 18, 1947, the army air force became the United States Air Force. Five months later, on February 16, 1948, the airfield was redesignated Robins Air Force Base. Robins received its first major tenant when the Fourteenth Air Force moved there from Orlando AFB, Florida.

The Berlin Airlift (1949) and the Korean War (1950–53) restored the workforce to 17,697 by December 1952. In addition to its normal mission, the depot returned most of the B-29s in storage to active service. During the war, Robins AFB overhauled and modified B-29 and F-84 aircraft as well as repairing F-80 and F-86 fighters. In 1951, the air force began a $3.5 million construction project. When this project reached completion in 1952, the air force made Robins AFB a permanent installation. Personnel strength grew in proportion and reached 17,697 by the end of 1952. A devastating F4 tornado struck the Warner Robins, Georgia area on April 30, 1953. Fortunately, the tornado struck immediately after the day shift had ended, and casualties were minimal. The base sustained $2 million in damage and one fatality, an officer's wife. All told, this one tornado caused the area nineteen fatalities, 350 injuries and $10 million in damage that left one thousand people homeless. This was the first tornado ever to be caught on film.

As the Korean War ended, along came a new conflict—the cold war. Robins AFB assumed the management of the Matador and later the Mace surface-to-surface missiles, as well as the Martin B-57 Canberra. To expedite services of Robins AFB to U.S. Air Force units all over the world, the Seventh Logistic Support Squadron was transferred to Robins AFB in October 1954 with C-124 Globemaster transport airplanes. In 1955, the air force added a new twelve-thousand-foot by three-hundred-foot all-weather runway to the airfield. By the end of the 1950s, Robins AFB had assumed management of virtually all the cargo aircraft in the air force, including the C-47, C-54, C-117, C-118, C-123, C-124 and C-130. As a result, Robins called itself the "cargo center of the air force." Also in the late 1950s, Robins added a Strategic Air Command base on the eastern side of the air force base. SAC units at Robins initially operated B-47 "Stratojets" before upgrading to B-52 "Stratofortresses."

When the U.S. Air Force closed down its maintenance depots at the former Brookley AFB in Mobile, Alabama, and the former Olmstead AFB in Middleton Township, Pennsylvania, Robins AFB assumed the workload of these depots. Some Robins AFB SAC units redeployed to Guam or Southeast Asia during the Vietnam War and took part in many of the bombing missions. Maintenance teams from Robins frequently traveled to Southeast Asia to repair severely damaged aircraft. Robins AFB eventually managed the Lockheed C-141, C-7 and the F-15 Eagle, as well as modifying the C-130s to the gunship configuration.

Robins played a key role in the Vietnam War (1964–73), supplying troops and materiel through the Southeast Asian pipeline and modifying AC-

119G/K and AC-130 gunships. Also playing a role were the C-141, the C-130, the C-123 and the C-124 cargo aircraft—all maintained at Robins. In 1973, these same C-141s supported the resupply of Israel in the Yom Kippur War. In October 1983, C-130s from Robins supported U.S. forces in the invasion of Grenada.

Between 1977 and 1981, Robins was the air base used by former president Jimmy Carter during his tenure on visits to his hometown of Plains. SAC's B-52s left Robins in 1983, and the Nineteenth Wing assumed solely a refueling mission with KC-135s.

In 1990–91, during the Persian Gulf War, Robins provided record numbers of parts, repairs and personnel to coalition forces in the Persian Gulf. Robins-maintained F-15 Eagles and the E-8 Joint STARS played key roles in defeating the Iraqi military powers. In March–June 1999, during Operation Allied Force, the same employees and weapon systems played a decisive role in defeating the forces of the Yugoslavian president Slobodan Milosevic.

In 1996, the Georgia Air National Guard's 116th Fighter Wing at Dobbins AFB relinquished its F-15 aircraft and moved to Robins, transitioning to B-1 Lancer bombers and being redesignated as the 116th Bomb Wing. That same year, the former 93rd Bomb Wing at Robins was reactivated as the 93rd Air Control Wing with the E-8 Joint STARS aircraft. In 2001, the B-1 bombers left Robins AFB, and the Georgia Air National Guard entered into a merged Active Guard "associate" wing arrangement in the Joint STARS mission with the active air force, with the Air National Guard holding lead responsibility as the 116th Air Control Wing.

In 2004, the Warner Robins Air Logistic Center and Robins AFB are jointly the largest single industrial complex in the state of Georgia. The twenty-three thousand civilian employees have an annual payroll over $1 billion. The Logistic Center manages and overhauls the F-15, C-141 Starlifter, C-5 Galaxy, C-130 Hercules and the AC-130 gunships—and all of the air force's helicopters. In addition, the center also supports the C-17 Globemaster III and U-2 aircraft.

Until June 2008, Robins was also the home of the KC-135s of the 19th Air Refueling Group, when the unit was deactivated, then reactivated a month later as the 19th Airlift Wing at Little Rock AFB, Arkansas. The E-8s of the 116th Air Control Wing continue to operate at Robins as a combined Regular Air Force and Georgia Air National Guard air control wing, and the headquarters of the Air Force Reserve Command is also located on the base. The metropolis of Warner Robins, Georgia, has grown in proportion to become the sixth largest city in Georgia, according to some ways of counting.

The C-27J schoolhouse, operated by L-3 Link, officially began classes at Robins Air Force Base, Georgia, in September 2008. L-3 Link (a subsidiary of L-3 Integrated Systems) operates the official C-27J schoolhouse at the Georgia Department of Defense's Fixed Wing Flight Facility at Robins AFB. This world-class flight facility includes training classrooms, a computer learning center, a large one-hundred-person auditorium with high-definition audiovisual equipment, flight planning and fight operations areas. The facility also houses the resident Government Flight Representative and Aviation Program Team assigned to the C-27J contract. Fixed-Wing Flight Facility Robins AFB is also home of Hotel Company, 171st Aviation Regiment, Georgia Army National Guard. H Company flies the C-23 Sherpa to support time-sensitive, mission critical cargo delivery to the warfighter.

Near the base is the Museum of Aviation. Begun in 1981, it has four major structures on forty-three acres and ninety historic aircraft. The museum is also home to the Georgia Aviation Hall of Fame, which honors outstanding Georgians prominent in aviation. The ninety-three aircraft and missiles on display include a B-52, SR-71, a Marietta, Georgia-built B-29 and a specially modified C-130 Hercules that was used in the failed Iran hostage rescue mission. It has become a major regional educational and historical resource that hosts more than 500,000 visitors annually.

THOMASVILLE ARMY AIR FIELD

During World War II, Thomasville Army Airfield was a United States Army Air Forces Third Air Force training base for reconnaissance and later fighter pilots. The 59th Reconnaissance Group flew P-39 Aircobras and P-40 Warhawks from the airfield from March 30, 1943, to May 1, 1944, providing combat training for replacement pilots before their deployment to the overseas combat theaters. Support organizations included the 1333rd Guard Squadron and 493rd Sub Depot. In 1944, all these units were replaced by the 339th AAF Base Unit (Combat Crew Training School, Fighter), which flew the P-51 Mustang. The military use of the airfield ended on September 30, 1945. Today it is known as the Thomasville Regional Airport, a public airport located four miles northeast of Thomasville, Georgia. The airport serves the general aviation community, with no scheduled commercial airline service.

Turner Air Force Base

In the summer of 1940, army air corps personnel from Maxwell AAF in Montgomery, Alabama, contacted the Albany Chamber of Commerce about the possibility of locating a training base at its community with the stipulation that the local government purchase the property. Anticipating the economic benefit to the area, the local government accepted the proposal.

The air corps looked at several sites, including the existing Albany Municipal Airport. The municipal airport eventually became the site of a primary contract pilot school (Albany Army Airfield). The air corps finally settled on a site four miles northeast of town in Dougherty County. The chamber of commerce raised $95,000 to purchase over 4,700 acres for the main base and four auxiliary fields in Lee County. When the army indicated that it desired an additional 200 acres for the main base, the city purchased the property outright. All of the land was then leased to the air corps for fifty-one per annum with a ninety-nine-year option.

There are still a few reminders of Turner Army Airfield near Albany, as evidenced by the abandoned World War II barracks and USAF signage.

Construction got underway on March 25, 1941, for the new training airfield. The immediate construction involved runways and airplane hangars, with three concrete runways, several taxiways and a large parking apron and a control tower. Several large hangars were also constructed. Buildings were ultimately utilitarian and quickly assembled. Most base buildings, not meant for long-term use, were constructed of temporary or semi-permanent materials. Although some hangars had steel frames and the occasional brick or tile brick building could be seen, most support buildings sat on concrete foundations but were of frame construction clad in little more than plywood and tarpaper.

Initially named the Albany Army Airfield, the base became Turner Army Airfield on July 21, 1941, in honor of Georgia native Lieutenant Sullivan Preston Turner, killed the year before as a result of a midair collision. It was activated on August 12, although the base was far from complete. In addition to the main base, Turner AAF had the following satellite airfields: Turner AAF Aux No. 1 (Leesburg Field), Turner AAF Aux No. 2 (West Smithville Field), Turner AAF Aux No. 3 (West Leesburg Field), Turner AAF Aux No. 4 (Albany Army Airfield), Turner AAF Aux No. 5 (Turf Field in Albany), Turner AAF Aux No. 6 (North Smithville Field), Turner AAF Aux No. 7 (Cordele Army Airfield), Turner AAF Aux No. 8 (Vidalia-Lyons Field) and Turner AAF Aux No. 9 (Tifton Army Airfield).

The Army Air Forces Flying Training Command, Southeast Training Center (later Eastern Flying Training Command) Seventy-fifth Flying Training Wing offered elementary and advanced training in two-engine aircraft at Turner Army Airfield during World War II. Turner was initially operated as a school for navigators. The initial core of navigators, slated to become instructors, received the training at Barksdale Field, Louisiana. In July 1941, fifteen navigator instructors arrived at Turner Field with the rank of cadet. For the next two months, the navigation instructors oversaw the construction of the navigation school while organizing a training syllabus. When navigation training began in September, the instructors were commissioned as second lieutenants.

The aircraft used exclusively for navigation training at Turner was the Beech AT-7, a modification of the C-45 Expeditor. The AT-7 carried three navigation students, each with a navigation table and instruments, an instructor and a pilot. Navigators received approximately one hundred hours of navigation training in the AT-7. In September 1942, the navigation school moved to Selman Field in Monroe, Louisiana.

Turner was also used during World War II to train Free French and Royal Air Force aircrews. By June 1942, training of British students resumed. At the end of the year, aircraft complement numbered thirty-three Curtiss AT-9s, eighty Cessna AT-17s, nine AT-6 Texans, seven BT-13 Valiants and a few miscellaneous types. In the fall of 1942, half of the AT-9s were removed and replaced with the Cessna AT-17 Bobcat. The AT-17 was a military version of Cessna Model T-50 with wooden wings, fabric-covered steel tube fuselage and fixed-pitch propellers. The AT-17 was described by pilots as having the characteristics of a twin-engine Cub. Although the AT-17 was one of the safest trainers, some instructors felt it lacked the performance to properly prepare students for the combat aircraft they would eventually fly.

To meet the army's immediate need for two-engine trainers, Beech Aircraft designed the AT-10 Wichita in 1940, with economy and ease of manufacture in mind. The aircraft was made of wood with the exception of the engine cowls and the cockpit enclosure. Even the fuel tanks were wood with a covering of neoprene rubber. The use of wood allowed Beech to subcontract the manufacture of many components to furniture manufacturers and other firms. The wooden construction resulted in a light aircraft with excellent performance—as long as both engines were running. Part of the AT-10's economy was achieved by providing the aircraft with propellers that could not be feathered. Therefore, if an AT-10 lost an engine, sustained flight depended on the temperature and aircraft weight. When an AT-10 peeled off from a formation flight at Moody and entered a high-speed dive, the fabric tore off the flight controls and the aircraft crashed, killing the pilots. Thereafter, the AT-10 was red-lined at 180 miles per hour.

During July 1944, Turner AAF began transitioning to the TB-25 Mitchell medium bomber for the twin-engine training role. In September, Turner received its first class of Free French students. In November 1944, aircraft complement stood at 183 TB-25s and 38 AT-10s, plus a few miscellaneous types. Turner also had a contingent of four WASP pilots that flew utility missions.

Turner was deactivated on August 15, 1946. Although inactive, Turner Field was under the control of the 2621st AAF Base Unit arrived from Barksdale Field, Louisiana, which acted as a caretaker unit. The airfield remained under the overall control of Army Air Force Training Command.

Turner Army Airfield was reactivated on April 1, 1947, and assigned to the Tactical Air Command's Ninth Air Force. A major renovation project was required to upgrade the temporary wooden facilities from their World War II configuration into a permanent air force base, involving the construction of concrete and brick buildings, along with rebuilding the runway to accommodate jet aircraft. On July 1, 1948, the airfield was renamed Turner Air Force Base as a result of the United States Air Force becoming a separate uniformed service.

The Thirty-first Fighter Wing was transferred without personnel or equipment to Turner on September 4, 1947, from Langley Field, Virginia. Initially flying North American P-51D (later F-51D) Mustangs, the wing trained to achieve tactical proficiency. In 1948, after the jet runway was completed at Turner, the wing was upgraded to the Republic F-84 Thunderjet.

The Thirty-first was redesignated as the Thirty-first Fighter-Bomber Wing on January 20, 1950, upon joining Strategic Air Command's Second Air Force and subsequently the Thirty-first Fighter Escort Wing on July 16, 1950, reflecting the wing's new mission to escort SAC's intercontinental Boeing B-29 and Boeing B-50 Stratofortress bomber fleet. Beginning in December 1950 through July 1951, all tactical and most support components deployed to England. Thereafter, it deployed to provide air defense in Japan during the Korean War from July to October 1952 and November 1953 to February 1954. The Thirty-first FEW earned an Air Force Outstanding Unit Award for making the first massed jet fighter crossing of the Pacific Ocean in July 1952. The wing was again redesignated as the Thirty-first Strategic Fighter Wing on January 20, 1953, as the escort mission within SAC became deemphasized.

On April 1, 1957, the Thirty-first was transferred to Tactical Air Command at Turner and was redesignated as the Thirty-first Fighter-Bomber Wing when re-equipped with the new North American F-100 Super Sabre aircraft. The wing rotated tactical components to Alaska in 1956 and 1957 and to Europe in 1958 and 1959. It became nonoperational at Turner on March 15, 1959, and was transferred to George Air Force Base, California.

A major expansion of the base in preparation for the arrival of B-52 bombers resulted in the airfield at Turner being greatly expanded into a configuration that was typical of a SAC B-52 base: a single twelve-thousand-foot runway with a parallel taxiway and a huge ramp area. Turner became the home of the Strategic Air Command's 4080th Strategic Reconnaissance Wing in 1957, resulting in extensive expansion of the primary runway and other facilities. One of the most significant aspects of the SAC expansion at Turner was the nearby installation of a ring of U.S. Army Nike Hercules surface-to-air missiles, which was a customary defensive shield for many B-52 bases. The Nikes were installed in two nearby off-base installations and were armed with nuclear warheads. Upon transfer of the 4080th SRW to

Laughlin AFB, Texas, in 1957, SAC established the 4138th Strategic Wing as the primary entity at Turner, operating B-52D Stratofortress and KC-135A Stratotanker aircraft. On January 1, 1959, SAC headquartered Eighth Air Force's 822nd Air Division at Turner.

On February 1, 1963, the 4138th SW was deactivated and all subordinate squadrons and B-52D and KC-135A aircraft assets transferred to the newly established 484th Bombardment Wing (Heavy). The 484th BW continued to maintain CONUS-based strategic nuclear alert responsibilities at Turner through the 1960s and deployed to Southeast Asia for most of 1966.

Turner began phasing down in 1966 in preparation for its transfer to the U.S. Navy when the 822nd Air Division was deactivated on September 2. The 484th BW was deactivated on March 25, 1967, and its aircraft assets were redistributed to other SAC units.

Turner was closed by the air force in 1967 and was turned over to the U.S. Navy. It then became Naval Air Station Albany (Turner Field) and housed ten squadrons of the navy's Reconnaissance Attack Wing ONE, operating the Mach 2 RA-5C Vigilante carrier-based reconnaissance aircraft, with the wing and squadrons relocating during 1967–68 from the then-closing NAS Sanford, Florida. Additional navy aircraft based at NAS Albany during this period included the TA-4F/TA-4J Skyhawk II and the TA-3B Skywarrior.

Turner was closed by the navy in 1976 and its RA-5C Vigilante wing and squadrons transferred to NAS Key West, Florida. At the time of its closure, the NAS Albany airfield consisted of a single runway (12,050 feet long by 300 feet wide), taxiways, a large ramp area and numerous hangars and buildings.

After its closure by the navy, Turner was briefly reused for civil flying and a tenant Georgia Army National Guard aviation unit, with the nearby Ayres aircraft manufacturing company using the field to train pilots for their crop-duster aircraft.

Following its closure, the site was actively marketed for economic redevelopment by the local government. They were rewarded by the selection in 1978 of the Turner AFB site by the Miller Brewing Company, which built an extensive brewery operation at the location. A large part of the base still exists. The brewery took the site from the runways east, but most of the base is still intact, including much of the signage along with many guard and utility shacks around the perimeter. Western concrete ramps are still there, as is much of the leftover hardware. The original perimeter chain-link fence is still up, and there are still signs warning against photography without permission of the commander. The site is now home to a U.S. Department of Labor Job Corps center.

FORT GORDON

The second Camp Gordon, named for Confederate lieutenant general John Brown Gordon, was activated for infantry and armor training during World War II near Augusta. During the war, its fifty-five thousand acres served as a divisional training base for the Fourth and Twenty-sixth Infantry Divisions and the Tenth Armored Division that fought in Europe in General George S. Patton's Third Army. (The inactivated Tenth Armored Division still calls Fort Gordon home.) Other facilities included a U.S. disciplinary barracks and, beginning in 1943, a prisoner of war camp for German and Italian World War II captives. After World War II, more than eighty-five thousand officers and enlisted personnel were discharged from Camp Gordon's Army Personnel Center.

Camp Gordon, almost deserted after June 1948, came to life in September 1948 with the establishment of the Signal Corps Training Center. The post's training mission grew with the addition of the Military Police School in September 1948 and the activation of the Engineer Aviation Unit Training Center in January 1949 (the latter remained at Camp Gordon for only one year).

The Korean conflict again placed Camp Gordon center stage in preparing soldiers for combat. In addition to communications personnel at the Signal

Looking down Sixth Avenue of Camp Gordon during World War II. *AdeQ Historical Archives*.

Seen here are the barracks (left) and signal towers (right) that comprised the U.S. Army Signal Training Center of Fort Gordon during the 1970s. *AdeQ Historical Archives.*

Corps Training Center and Signal Unit Training Group, MPs trained for combat assignments while the Fifty-first Antiaircraft Artillery Brigade formed three detachments before moving to Camp Stewart, Georgia. In 1950, the installation became the site for military government training for the army.

Also during the decade, Camp Gordon was home to the only army criminal investigation laboratory in the continental United States, as well as a rehabilitation training center and a U.S. disciplinary barracks. In 1953, the Basic Replacement Training Center and the Advanced Leader's School provided basic training and advanced leadership training (both were inactivated in 1955). The Civil Affairs School arrived in 1955 as part of the Civil Affairs and Military Government School. Camp Gordon, becoming a permanent army installation on March 21, 1956, was redesignated Fort Gordon.

The U.S. Army Training Center (Basic) was activated here in 1957. During the Vietnam War, infantry, military police and signal soldiers trained at Fort Gordon. While signal corps training continued to expand throughout the 1960s, other activities ceased through postwar deactivations and the Military Police School's move to Fort McClellan, Alabama. In June 1962, all activities of the Signal Corps Training Center were reorganized under the U.S. Army Southeastern Signal School.

During the Vietnam War, Fort Gordon was home to Camp Crocket, an area of the post conducting eight-week infantry training courses for soldiers in line to attend airborne training at Fort Benning, Georgia, and then be assigned to airborne units in Vietnam. The location closed as the war ended, and today the site is overgrown with pine trees. In addition, approximately 2,200 signal officers were trained at Fort Gordon's Signal Officer Candidate School (OCS), before all U.S. Army branch OCSs were merged with the Infantry OCS at Fort Benning, Georgia. During the war, Fort Gordon was also a training location for Military Police Corps in the Brems Barracks region of the fort, which was also later used in the 1980s for training radioteletype operators. Designating the installation the U.S. Army Signal Center and Fort Gordon, the army consolidated all communications training at Fort Gordon on October 1, 1974. The arrival of the army's Computer Science School was only part of the impetus for the fort's tremendous growth during the 1980s.

The following decade found its Mobilization Command deploying numerous troops to Southwest Asia during Operation Desert Shield–Desert Storm (1990–91). Fort Gordon figures prominently in the post–cold war national defense. Still the "Home of the Signal Regiment," it also supports the 35th Signal Brigade, 513th Military Intelligence Brigade, the National Security Agency/Central Security Service Georgia and the 7th Signal Command (Theater).

NAVAL SUBMARINE BASE KINGS BAY

This is the newest military facility established in Georgia in the latter part of the twentieth century. The army began to acquire land at Kings Bay in 1954 to build a military ocean terminal to ship ammunition in case of a national emergency. Construction actively began in 1956 and was completed in 1958. Since there was no immediate operational need for the installation, it was placed in an inactive ready status. The most prominent feature of the terminal was the two-thousand-foot-long, eighty-seven-foot-wide concrete and steel wharf. In addition, three parallel railroad tracks would have enabled the simultaneous loading of several ammunition ships from rail cars and trucks.

Elsewhere aboard the base, the army built forty-seven miles of railroad tracks. Spurs off the main line ran into temporary storage areas that were protected by earthen barricades. These mounds of dirt, still prominent

The preserved sail of the USS *George Bancroft* (SSBN-643) prominently marks the entrance to Naval Submarine Base Kings Bay in southeastern Georgia.

features in many areas of the base, were designed to localize damage in case of explosive accidents. Never activated to serve its primary purpose, the army base was used for other missions. In 1964, as Hurricane Dora hammered the area, nearly 100 area residents were sheltered aboard at the base. Also, during the Cuban missile crisis, an army transportation battalion of 1,100 personnel and seventy small boats took up position at Kings Bay.

The chain of events that led to today's combination of high-tempo submarine operations at Kings Bay and the complex construction project that reshaped the face of thousands of acres of land began in 1975. At the time, treaty negotiations between Spain and the United States were in progress. A proposed change to our base agreement with Spain was the withdrawal of the fleet ballistic-missile submarine squadron, Submarine Squadron 16, from its operational base at Rota, Spain. Anticipating that this would take place, the chief of naval operations ordered studies to select a new refit site on the East Coast. In January 1976, negotiators initialed a draft treaty between Spain and the United States; it called for withdrawal of the squadron from Rota by July 1979. The U.S. Congress ratified the treaty in June 1976. A site-selection steering group evaluated more than sixty sites along the Atlantic and Gulf coasts. By the summer of 1976, the number of sites was narrowed to five: Narragansett Bay, Rhode Island; Cheatham Annex, Virginia; Charleston, South Carolina; Kings Bay, Georgia; and Mosquito Lagoon, Florida.

A comprehensive study evaluated each site against a number of criteria, including costs, ability to meet required schedule, land availability to meet explosive safety requirements, operational capabilities, logistics consideration, environmental impact and growth potential for future requirements. After careful review, the navy selected Kings Bay. The first navy personnel arrived in the Kings Bay area in January 1978 and started preparations for the orderly transfer of property from the army to the navy. Naval Submarine Support Base Kings Bay was established in a developmental status on July 1, 1978.

The base, now Naval Submarine Base Kings Bay, occupies the entire former army terminal, as well as several thousand additional acres. Preparations for the arrival of the submarine squadron went forward in haste throughout the remainder of 1978 and into 1979. Commander Submarine Squadron 16 greeted the submarine tender USS *Simon Lake* (AS-33) when it arrived at Kings Bay on July 2, 1979. Four days later, USS *James Monroe* (SSBN 622) entered Kings Bay and moored alongside *Simon Lake* to begin a routine refit in preparation for another deterrent patrol. Kings Bay has been an operating submarine base since that day.

In May 1979, the navy selected Kings Bay as the preferred East Coast site for the Ohio-class submarine. On October 23, 1980, after a one-year environmental impact study was completed and with congressional approval, the secretary of the navy announced Kings Bay as the future home of the new Trident submarine. The building project included the construction of three major commands: Trident Training Facility (TTF), Trident Refit Facility (TRF) and Strategic Weapons Facility, Atlantic (SWFLANT). On January 15, 1989, the first Trident submarine, USS *Tennessee* (SSBN 734), arrived at Kings Bay. The commissioning of USS *Louisiana* (SSBN 742) in September 1997 gave Kings Bay its full complement of ten Trident submarines. The enormous effort put forth by all the commands at Kings Bay reached fruition in late March 1990, when the Trident II (D-5) missile made its first deterrent patrol on board *Tennessee*.

The end of the cold war and the reorganization of military forces in the 1990s affected Kings Bay. A nuclear policy review recommended the navy reduce the Ohio-class fleet ballistic-missile submarines from eighteen to fourteen by 2005. In order to meet the review recommendation, the four oldest Ohio-class submarines were decommissioned and converted to guided missile (SSGN) platforms. *Pennsylvania, Kentucky, Nebraska, Maine* and *Louisiana* shifted homeport to Naval Base Kitsap, Washington, as part of balancing the Trident fleet.

USS *Florida* (SSGN 728) arrived at Kings Bay in May 2006 and the USS *Georgia* (SSGN 729) in 2007.

Currently assigned to Kings Bay (2011):
Ballistic Missile Submarines
USS *Maryland* (SSBN 738)
USS *Rhode Island* (SSBN 740)
USS *Tennessee* (SSBN 734)
USS *West Virginia* (SSBN 736)
USS *Wyoming* (SSBN 742)
USS *Alaska* (SSBN 732)

Guided Missile Submarines:
USS *Florida* (SSGN 728)
USS *Georgia* (SSGN 729)

BIBLIOGRAPHY

Adams, James Mack. *A History of Fort Screven Georgia.* Tybee Island, GA: JMA2 Publications, 1996.

Alexander, Jerry Lamar. *Blood Red Runs the Sacred Keowe: 1760's Cherokee War Against British in Carolinas, Georgia & Tennessee Mountains!* Seneca, SC: self-published, 2009.

Associated Press, "Archeologists Find Relics at Georgia Fort: Final Battle of War of 1812 Fought at Point Peter." May 20, 2005. www.msnbc.msn.com/id/7923142/ns/technology_and_science-science.

Byous, Jim. "The Fortresses of Savannah." Savannah Images Project, website of Armstrong Atlantic State University. www.sip.armstrong.edu/Forts/Essay.html.

Chapman, James H., and Leland G. Ferguson. *Frontiers in the Soil: The Archeology of Georgia.* Athens: Carl Vinson Institute of Government, University of Georgia, 2003. Reprint of the 1979 edition published by Frontiers Publishing Company.

Christian, William E. *Undaunted: The History of Fort McAllister, Georgia.* Darien, GA: Darien Printing & Graphics, 1996.

Conner, Judson J. *Muskets, Knives and Bloody Marshes: The Fight for Colonial Georgia.* St. Simons Island, GA: Saltmarsh Press, Inc., 2001.

Cook, Jeannine. *Fort King George: Step One to Statehood.* Darien, GA: Darien News, 1990.

de Quesada, Alejandro M. *A History of Florida's Forts: Florida's Lonely Outposts.* Charleston, SC: The History Press, 2006.

———. *The Men of Fort Foster.* Union City, TN: Pioneer Press, 1994.

———. *Spanish Colonial Fortifications in North America, 1565–1822*. London: Osprey Publishing, 2010.

Durham, Roger S. *Fort McAllister*. Charleston, SC: Arcadia Publishing, 2004.

———. *Guardian of Savannah: Fort McAllister, Georgia, in the Civil War and Beyond*. Columbia: University of South Carolina Press, 2008.

Elliott, Daniel T. *Argyle: Colonial Fort on the Ogeechee*. Fort Stewart, GA: United States Department of Defense Legacy Resource Management Program, 1997.

———. *Ebenezer and Sunbury: Revolutionary War Landscapes of Two Dead Towns in Georgia*. Savannah, GA: LAMAR Institute, Inc., 2010.

Gaines, William C. "Second System Fortification Construction at Savannah, Georgia, 1807–1815." *Journal of America's Military Past* 27, no. 2 (Fall 2000): 19–39.

Gillmore, Q.A., Brig. Gen. (U.S. Vols.). *Official Report to the United States Engineer Department of the Siege and Reduction of Fort Pulaski, Georgia, February, March, and April 1862*. New York: D. Van Nostrand, 1862.

Guss, John Walker. *Fortresses of Savannah, Georgia*. Charleston, SC: Arcadia Publishing, 2002.

Ivers, Larry E. *British Drums on the Southern Frontier: The Military Colonization of Georgia, 1733–1749*. Chapel Hill: University of North Carolina Press, 1974.

Johnson, James M. *Militiamen, Rangers, and Redcoats: The Military in Georgia, 1754–1776*. Macon, GA: Mercer University Press, 1992.

Jones, C.C. *Dead Towns of Georgia*. Savannah, GA: Oglethorpe Press, Inc., 1997.

"Journal of an Expedition against the Rebels of Georgia in North America Under Orders of Archibald Campbell Esquire Lieut. Colol. of His Majesty's 71st Regimt. 1778." Printed for Richmond County Historical Society. Darien, GA: Ashantilly Press, 1981.

Lewis, Bessie. "Old Fort King George." N.p.: Left Bank Art Gallery, 2004. Previously published in the October–November 1967 issue of *Georgia Magazine*.

Marlin, L.G. *The Fort Yargo Epic*. Winder, GA: Winder News Publishing Co., 1960.

Miles, Jim. *Georgia Civil War Sites*. Warner Robins, GA: J&R Graphics, 1987.

Miller, Francis Trevelyan, editor in chief. *The Photographic History of the Civil War: Volume Five, Forts and Artillery*. New York: Review of Reviews Co., 1911.

Moore, Steve, Ranger, NPS. *Frederica, Fort and Town: Historical Background*. Washington, D.C.: Government Printing Office, April 11, 2006.

Neuhauser, Hans. *Fort Screven (1897–1945): A Tour of Georgia's Historic Coastal Fort.* Tybee Island, GA: Tybee Island Historical Society, 1988.

Rains, George W. *History of the Confederate Powder Works.* Nashville, GA: Wayne and Judy Dasher, 2008. Reprint of the 1882 article from the *Newburgh Daily News Print*, Newburgh, NY.

Reese, Trevor R. *Frederica: Colonial Fort and Town—Its Place in History.* St. Simons Island, GA: Fort Frederica Association, 1969.

Ridley, William E., Col., USAF (Ret.). *Georgia Air National Guard History, 1941–2000.* Charlotte, NC: Fine Books Publishing Company, 2000.

Roberts Robert B. *Encyclopedia of Historic Forts: The Military, Pioneer, and Trading Posts of the United States.* New York: Macmillan Publishing Company, 1988.

Robins Air Force Base Heritage Committee. *A Pictorial History of Robins Air Force Base, Georgia.* Macon, GA: University Press of the South, 1982.

Schiller, Herbert M. *Fort Pulaski and the Defense of Savannah.* N.p.: Eastern National, 1997.

Scruggs, Carroll Proctor. *Georgia During the Revolution.* Norcross, GA: Bay Tree Grove, Publishers, 1975.

Stilson, Harold A. (Sgt., USA), Thomas E. Crolely (St. Sgt., USA) and John W. Halley (Cpl., USA), eds. *Pictorial Review of the Five Eleven.* Camp Mackall, NC: Engineer Reproduction and Publications Section, Airborne Command, 1943.

Walker, Robert Sparks. *Torchlights to the Cherokees.* Johnson City, TN: Overmountain Press, 1993. Reprint of the 1931 edition published by MacMillan Company.

AUTHOR'S NOTE: Another fantastic quick reference on forts in Georgia as well as throughout the United States is a website with data compiled by Pete and/or Phil Payette solely dedicated to this area of study: "North American Forts, 1526–1956—A Catalogue and Gazetteer of Forts and Fortresses, Frontier Posts, Camps, Stockades, Blockhouses, Garrisons, Arsenals, and Seacoast Batteries in the United States and Canada and Associated Territories" (www.northamericanforts.com).

INDEX

A

Albany Army Airfield 116, 117
Andersonville Prison 68, 69, 71, 72, 73, 77, 78, 79
Atlanta
  city of 46, 67, 72, 73, 75, 76, 77, 83, 101, 116, 124
  Civil War defenses 73, 75, 76, 77, 83, 101, 116
Augusta Arsenal 51, 52

B

Bainbridge Army Airfield 126, 127
Battery Backus 88
Battery Daniels 65
Battery Garland 88
Battery Hambright 89
Battery Rose Dew 65
Battery Stephens 65
Beaulieu Battery 65
Blackshear Confederate Prison Camp 79
Byron Field 121, 122, 133

C

Camp Crawford 54
Camp Gordon (Atlanta) 101, 102, 116
Camp Gordon (Augusta). See Fort Gordon
Camp Hancock 100
Camp Jesup 84
Camp Lawton 77, 78, 79
Camp Recovery 54, 56, 57
Camp Stewart. See Fort Stewart
Camp Sumter 68, 69, 70, 71, 77
Camp Thomas 92, 94
Camp Toccoa 118, 119, 120
Camp Wheeler 96, 97, 98, 99, 100, 131
Chatham Army Airfield 127
Cochran Army Airfield 120
Confederate Battery (Jekyll Island) 61, 65, 76
Confederate Powder Works 51, 53

D

Dublin Temporary Prisoner of War Camp 99

E

Eagle Tavern 35
East "Dummy" Fort (Savannah) 91
Ebenezer
   Revolutionary War fortifications
     25, 26
   town of 13, 25, 26, 27

F

Federal Fort (Bartow County) 73
Fort Argyle 13, 14
Fort Augusta 21, 22, 23
Fort Barrington 21
Fort Bartow 65
Fort Beauregard 64
Fort Benjamin Hawkins. *See* Fort
   Hawkins
Fort Benning 102, 103, 104, 105,
   106, 107, 119, 145
Fort Boggs 62, 65
Fort Buffington 59
Fort Cornwallis 21, 23
Fort Daniel 46
Fort Darien 23, 24
Fort Early 44
Fort Edwards 35
Fort Frederica 14, 15, 16, 17, 18
Fort Gaines
   antebellum era 47, 48, 49
   Civil War era 67, 68, 69
Fort George 31
Fort Gilmer 59
Fort Gordon 143, 144, 145
Fort Hawkins 40, 41, 42
Fort Hollingsworth 36, 37
Fort Hughes 55, 56
Fort Jackson. *See* Fort James Jackson
Fort James Jackson 42, 44
Fort King George 12, 13, 14
Fort Mathews 39
Fort McAllister 65, 66, 67

Fort McIntosh 24
Fort McPherson 83, 84, 85, 86, 124
Fort Mitchell (AL) 46, 47, 48
Fort Morris 27, 28
Fort Oglethorpe 44, 92, 93, 94, 95,
   96
Fort Peachtree 45, 46
Fort Peter 39, 40
Fort Prevost 28, 29, 33, 34
Fort Pulaski 9, 10, 44, 57, 58, 59,
   62, 89
Fort Savannah 28
Fort Scott 53, 54, 55, 56, 57
Fort Screven 50, 87, 92
Fort Smith (AR) 54
Fort Stewart 14, 107, 110, 111,
   112, 114, 115
Fort Tattnall 65
Fort Thunderbolt 64, 65
Fort Toulouse 13
Fort Tyler 79, 80, 81
Fort Walker 73, 74, 75
Fort Wayne 30, 33, 34
Fort Wimberly 30, 65
Fort Yargo 38
Forty-eighth New York State
     Volunteer Infantry
     Regimental band 58

H

Hunter Army Airfield 113

M

Martello Tower 49, 50
McPherson Barracks 83, 85
Mission de San José de Zapala 12
Mission Nuestra Señora de
     Guadalupe de Tolomato 11
Mission Santa Catalina de Guale 11
Moody Air Force Base 124, 125,
   126

N

Naval Submarine Base Kings Bay
145, 146, 147

P

Peachtree Street Fort 74

R

R-28 Nike Missile Base 133
R-88 Nike Missile Base 133
Robins Air Force Base 131, 132,
134, 137
Robins Field 131

S

San Miguel de Gualdape 11
Sapelo Island Presidio 11, 12
Savannah
ANGB 131
city of 9, 13, 14, 20, 21, 30, 33,
42, 44, 59, 61, 62, 67, 78,
113, 114, 128
Civil War fortifications 43, 62, 65,
67, 112
Revolutionary War fortifications
13, 14, 25, 26, 28, 30, 31
Savannah Volunteer Guards
armory 90
East "Dummy" Fort 91
West "Dummy" Fort 91
Spring Hill Redoubt 29, 30
Star Fort (Camp Sumter/
Andersonville Prison) 70,
71
St. Catherines Island Presidio 11

T

Thomasville Army Airfield 137
Tolomato Presidio 11
TU-28 Nike Missile Base 133

TU-79 Nike Missile Base 133
Turner Air Force Base 138, 141

U

USS George Bancroft 146

W

Welleston Air Depot 131, 132
West "Dummy" Fort 91
Wormsloe Plantation 18, 19, 30

About the Author

Alejandro de Quesada is a Florida-based military history writer, an experienced researcher and a collector of militaria, photos and documents. He runs a firearms company as well as an archive and historical consultancy for museums and films as a secondary business. Alejandro has written over one hundred articles and over thirty books, including several for The History Press, and is the author of the following titles to date: *A History of Florida's Forts* and *Spanish Colonial Fortifications in North America*.

Visit us at
www.historypress.net

CPSIA information can be obtained
at www.ICGtesting.com
Printed in the USA
BVHW052245291121
622778BV00003B/300

9 781540 205636